JUVENILE INJUSTICE:

Police abuse and detention of street children in Kenya

Human Rights Watch Children's Rights Project

Human Rights Watch
New York · Washington · London · Brussels

Copyright © June 1997 by Human Rights Watch
All rights reserved.
Printed in the United States of America.

ISBN 1-56432-214-9
Library of Congress Catalog Card Number 97-77536

Cover photograph by Yodon Thonden, street boys in Nairobi, Kenya.

Human Rights Watch Children's Rights Project
The Human Rights Watch Children's Rights Project was established in 1994 to monitor and promote the human rights of children around the world. Lois Whitman is the director; Yodon Thonden is counsel; Rosa Erenreich and Lee Tucker are consultants; and Linda Shipley is the associate. Jane Green Schaller is chair of the Advisory committee.

Addresses for Human Rights Watch
485 Fifth Avenue, New York, NY 10017-6104
Tel: (212) 972-8400, Fax: (212) 972-0905, E-mail: hrwnyc@hrw.org

1522 K Street, N.W., #910, Washington, DC 20005-1202
Tel: (202) 371-6592, Fax: (202) 371-0124, E-mail: hrwdc@hrw.org

33 Islington High Street, N1 9LH London, UK
Tel: (171) 713-1995, Fax: (171) 713-1800, E-mail: hrwatchuk@gn.apc.org

15 Rue Van Campenhout, 1000 Brussels, Belgium
Tel: (2) 732-2009, Fax: (2) 732-0471, E-mail: hrwatcheu@gn.apc.org

Web Site Address: http://www.hrw.org
Gopher Address://gopher.humanrights.org:5000/11/int/hrw
Listserv address: To subscribe to the list, send an e-mail message to majordomo@igc.apc.org with "subscribe hrw-news" in the body of the message (leave the subject line blank).

HUMAN RIGHTS WATCH

Human Rights Watch conducts regular, systematic investigations of human rights abuses in some seventy countries around the world. Our reputation for timely, reliable disclosures has made us an essential source of information for those concerned with human rights. We address the human rights practices of governments of all political stripes, of all geopolitical alignments, and of all ethnic and religious persuasions. Human Rights Watch defends freedom of thought and expression, due process and equal protection of the law, and a vigorous civil society; we document and denounce murders, disappearances, torture, arbitrary imprisonment, discrimination, and other abuses of internationally recognized human rights. Our goal is to hold governments accountable if they transgress the rights of their people.

Human Rights Watch began in 1978 with the founding of its Helsinki division. Today, it includes five divisions covering Africa, the Americas, Asia, the Middle East, as well as the signatories of the Helsinki accords. It also includes three collaborative projects on arms transfers, children's rights, and women's rights. It maintains offices in New York, Washington, Los Angeles, London, Brussels, Moscow, Dushanbe, Rio de Janeiro, and Hong Kong. Human Rights Watch is an independent, nongovernmental organization, supported by contributions from private individuals and foundations worldwide. It accepts no government funds, directly or indirectly.

The staff includes Kenneth Roth, executive director; Michele Alexander, development director; Cynthia Brown, program director; Holly J. Burkhalter, advocacy director; Barbara Guglielmo, finance and administration director; Robert Kimzey, publications director; Jeri Laber, special advisor; Lotte Leicht, Brussels office director; Susan Osnos, communications director; Jemera Rone, counsel; Wilder Tayler, general counsel; and Joanna Weschler, United Nations representative.

The regional directors of Human Rights Watch are Peter Takirambudde, Africa; José Miguel Vivanco, Americas; Sidney Jones, Asia; Holly Cartner, Helsinki; and Eric Goldstein, Middle East (acting). The project directors are Joost R. Hiltermann, Arms Project; Lois Whitman, Children's Rights Project; and Dorothy Q. Thomas, Women's Rights Project.

The members of the board of directors are Robert L. Bernstein, chair; Adrian W. DeWind, vice chair; Roland Algrant, Lisa Anderson, William Carmichael, Dorothy Cullman, Gina Despres, Irene Diamond, Fiona Druckenmiller, Edith Everett, Jonathan Fanton, James C. Goodale, Jack Greenberg, Vartan Gregorian, Alice H. Henkin, Stephen L. Kass, Marina Pinto Kaufman, Bruce Klatsky, Harold Hongju Koh, Alexander MacGregor, Josh Mailman, Samuel K. Murumba, Andrew Nathan, Jane Olson, Peter Osnos, Kathleen Peratis, Bruce Rabb, Sigrid Rausing, Anita Roddick, Orville Schell, Sid Sheinberg, Gary G. Sick, Malcolm Smith, Domna Stanton, Nahid Toubia, Maureen White, Rosalind C. Whitehead, and Maya Wiley.

ACKNOWLEDGMENTS

Research for this report was undertaken in Kenya by Yodon Thonden, counsel to Human Rights Watch Children's Rights Project. The report was written by Yodon Thonden and edited by Lois Whitman, director of Human Rights Watch Children's Rights Project, and Binaifer Nowrojee, counsel to Human Rights Watch/Africa. Production assistance was provided by Linda Shipley, Human Rights Watch Children's Rights Project associate.

We wish to express our gratitude to the many organizations and individuals in Kenya who helped make this report possible. We especially would like to thank Elizabeth Oyugi, Villoo Nowrojee, Lee Muthoga, and Dorcas Buku of ANPPCAN Kenya, who generously gave their time and assistance to us in planning and conducting our fact-finding mission. We also would like to thank Mr. S. Ole Kwallah, the director of the Children's Department (Ministry of Home Affairs), for his cooperation in our work. We thank the many nongovernmental organizations and their representatives with whom we met, including Pandipieri Street Children Programme, Rescue Dada Center, Child Welfare Society of Kenya, the Undugu Society of Kenya, the Kenya Alliance for the Advancement of Children, Mji Wa Salama, Kituo Cha Sheria, and the Kenya Human Rights Commission and the many other individuals and their organizations that asked not to be identified. Finally, our heartfelt thanks go to the many boys and girls who talked freely with us and whose names have been changed in this report for their safety.

I. INTRODUCTION 1
    Summary 1
    Recommendations 6
        To the Kenyan government 6
        To the United Nations 12
        To Donor Country Governments 12
        To NGOs 13

II. BACKGROUND 14
    The Growing Presence of Street Children 14

III. POLICE ABUSES AGAINST STREET CHILDREN 21
    International and Kenyan Standards 22
    Police Abuse of Children on the Streets 23
        Categories of Law Enforcement Personnel 23
        Physical Abuse on the Streets 25
        Extortion 26
        Sexual Abuse of Street Girls 27
        Use of Deadly Force 28
    Police Accountability 30

IV. ARBITRARY DETENTION 34
    International and Kenyan Standards 35
    Confinement in Police Lockups 37
        Physical Abuse by Police 39
        Physical Conditions in Lockups 42
        Children Held with Adults 45

V. PROCEDURES FOR CONFINING
    STREET CHILDREN IN INSTITUTIONS 48
    Juvenile Court 48
    Jurisdiction of Juvenile Court 51
    Referral of Cases to Juvenile Court 53
    Rights of the Accused 54
        International and Kenyan Standards 54
        Kenyan Practice 56
    Committal to Remand Detention 62
    Disposition of Cases: Sentencing 66

VI. CONDITIONS IN INSTITUTIONS TO WHICH
     CHILDREN ARE COMMITTED 71
     International Standards 71
     Remand Institutions 74
          Juvenile Remand Homes 74
          Adult Remand Prisons 80
     Approved Schools 84
          Mixing of Children 85
          Physical Conditions 86
          Education and Vocational Training 87
          Discipline and Punishment 88
     Borstal Institutions 90
          Mixing of Children 91
          Physical Conditions 92
          Education and Vocational Training 93
          Discipline and Punishment 95
          Grievance Procedures 97
          Discharge 99
     Prisons 99

VII. THE CHILDREN ACT 102

VIII. CONCLUSION 106

APPENDICES 108
     APPENDIX A:
          Excerpts from the U.N. Convention on
          the Rights Of the Child 109
     APPENDIX B:
          U.N. Standard Minimum Rules For the
          Administration of Juvenile Justice 118
     APPENDIX C:
          U.N. Rules for the Protection Of
          Juveniles Deprived of Their Liberty 128
     APPENDIX D:
          U.N. Code of Conduct for Law Enforcement Officials ... 143
     APPENDIX E:
          U.N. Basic Principles on the Use Of Force and
          Firearms by Law Enforcement Officials 149

GLOSSARY OF TERMS AND ABBREVIATIONS

Afande	Kiswahili term of respect for police.
ANNPCAN	African Network for the Prevention and Protection against Child Abuse and Neglect.
Approved officer	Individuals appointed by voluntary organizations who are approved" or "gazetted" by the minister of home affairs to work on issues related to the protection and care of children.
Approved school	Correctional institution, under the administration of the Children's Department, to which children ten years old and above may be committed by courts.
Askari	Kiswahili word for guard or soldier.
Beijing Rules	U.N. Standard Minimum Rules for the Administration of Juvenile Justice.
Borstal institution	Correctional institution, under the administration of the Prisons Department, to which children fifteen years old and above may be committed after being found guilty of criminal offenses.
CID	Criminal Investigation Department of the police.
Children's officer	Staff member of the Children's Department, authorized to refer cases of children "in need of protection or discipline" to court and to make recommendations to court on what correctional measure to order in a "protection or discipline" case.
ICCPR	International Covenant on Civil and Political Rights.
Juvenile remand home	Temporary detention center, under administration of the Children's Department, to which children are committed by court pendingadjudication or final disposition of their cases.
KANU	Kenya African National Union.

NGO	Nongovernmental organization.
P&C	Protection and care, used to refer to a subcategory of children who fall within the broader category of children "in need of protection or discipline."
P&D	Protection and discipline, used to refer to a subcategory of children who fall within the broader category of children "in need of protection or discipline."
Probation officer	Staff member of the Probation and After Care Services Department, authorized to make recommendation to court on correctional measures to order in a child's criminal case.
Remand prison	Temporary detention center, under administration of Prisons Department, to which adults and children fourteen years old and above are committed by court pending adjudication or final disposition of their cases.
Reservist	Police reserve officer, employed on a part-time basis to perform regular police duties.
Shamba	Farm.
Sukuma wiki	Green leafy vegetable.
U.N. Rules for the Protection of Juveniles	U.N. Rules for the Protection of Juveniles Deprived of their Liberty.
Ugali	Stiff porridge made of maize meal.

I. INTRODUCTION

Summary

Street children in Kenya face innumerable hardships and danger in their daily lives. In addition to the hazards of living on the street, these children face harassment and abuse from the police and within the juvenile justice system for no reason other than the fact that they are street children. Living outside the protection of responsible adults, street children are easy and silent targets for abuse by police and society at large. On the streets, they are subject to frequent beatings by police as well as monetary extortion and sexual abuse. They are subject to frequent arrest simply because they are homeless; "vagrancy"[1] (being without a fixed abode) is a criminal offense under Kenyan law. Once arrested, often by plainclothes police in roundup operations, street children are processed through the revolving doors of the Kenyan juvenile justice system, where children pass back and forth between remand detention centers and court before a final disposition is reached in their cases. After spending indefinite periods of time on remand, where they are further neglected and abused, they may be finally sentenced to institutions called approved schools, borstal institutions or adult prisons, which do little to improve their lives. Further, the procedures by which street children are deprived of their liberty and are committed to these institutions do not comply with the due process standards of international law. This report documents the treatment of street children by the Kenyan police, and in the juvenile justice system as a whole, following street children from an all too frequent route from street to police station lockup, from lockup to court, from court to detention in remand institutions, and finally from remand to confinement in correctional institutions.

For the purpose of this report, Human Rights Watch undertook a fact-finding mission to Kenya, in September and October of 1996. We interviewed over sixty children in Nairobi, Kisumu and Mombasa. Most interviews with children were conducted with the assistance of interpreters on the streets, or in shelters for street children and, in certain cases, in correctional or remand institutions where children were confined. Additionally we interviewed members of nongovernmental organizations (NGOs) and human rights activists that work with street children in Kenya. A number of the NGO representatives we spoke with requested anonymity for themselves and their organizations, particularly when speaking on issues of police abuse of street children, reflecting the sensitive nature of the issues involved and the fear that nongovernmental actors have of the

---

[1] Vagrancy Act, Chapter 58 of the Laws of Kenya.

government and police. We also met with government officials, including representatives and staff of the Children's Department, the Probation and After-Care Services Department, the police and the judiciary. Additionally, we visited three juvenile remand homes and three approved schools, and interviewed staff there. We also observed proceedings at the Juvenile Law Court in Nairobi.

Upwards of 40,000 street children live in Kenya today, with over half of their population concentrated in the capital, Nairobi. Numerous and complex socio-economic factors have fueled the rising presence of children on the streets, including, but not limited to: rapid urbanization and the breakdown of traditional support structures of the African extended family; the increasingly difficult circumstances of women as heads of single-parent households; the inability of parents to pay uniform and book fees, and other costs of public education; the displacement of large numbers of people in urban slum clearance operations, sometimes leaving families homeless overnight; and, in recent years, the internal displacement of an estimated 300,000 people, including a high percentage of children, from state-sponsored "ethnic" violence in the west and Rift Valley of Kenya.

Some street children we spoke with had parents or family members in nearby slum areas or in faraway villages, with whom they maintained some contact. Some were not actually "homeless" but spent periods of varying length on the street before returning to their homes, and then returned back to the streets. Most said they came from single-parent households or that they had lived with a relative other than a parent before leaving home. Some were abandoned or orphaned; others left their families and homes of their own accord citing the inability of their families to provide and care for them, or problems in their relationships with their parents, as the cause. Thus when we use the term "street children" we refer to the broad spectrum of children "for whom the street more than their family has become their real home."[2]

---

[2] This definition of street children was formulated by the Inter-NGO Programme for Street Children and Street Youth, cited in Judith Ennew, *Street and Working Children: A Guide to Planning* (London: Save the Children, 1994), p. 15. The full definition is as follows: "Street children are those for whom the street (in the widest sense of the word: i.e. unoccupied dwellings, wasteland etc.) more than their family has become their real home, a situation in which there is no protection, supervision or direction from responsible adults." It should be noted that UNICEF has suggested a distinction between children *on* the streets and children *of* the streets. Children *on* the streets are children who still maintain close ties to their families and return to their family homes in the evenings, while spending their days on the streets. Children *of* the street are children whose ties to their families have been severed, and who often actually sleep on the street and struggle alone for survival. *Street*

Arrest and Confinement of Children in Correctional Institutions

With their numbers on the rise, police and local government authorities are increasingly at a loss as to what to do with street children. Despite the emergence, on the surface, of coalitions of NGOs working on issues related to street children, including the establishment of the National Task Force on Street Children (to advise the government at the cabinet level on issues related to street children), and a stated commitment of the attorney general to addressing the needs of street children, the reality is that street children continue to be criminalized in Kenya simply because they are homeless. Government response to the rising presence of street children is to arrest and charge street children with the crime of "vagrancy."

Law enforcement officials who police the streets and carry out arrests of street children demonstrate brutal attitudes towards street children and abuse and exploit the children with impunity. Children reported that on the street they are often harassed and beaten by police, and have to pay bribes to police in order to avoid arrest. Street girls reported being sexually propositioned by police in order to avoid arrest or to be released from custody, including raped.

Often regarded by police as petty criminals, or vagrants at best, street children are often rounded up, for no reason other than the fact that they are on the streets. Although police and government officials may state that street children are rounded up for the alleged purposes of identifying and reuniting children with their families or placing them in appropriate institutions for their care, the manner in which the children are subsequently treated, both by police and within institutions, belies such intentions; these children are arrested and dealt with as criminals.

Police roundups are conducted with brute force and with little regard for the welfare of the children, who are often taunted, scolded, manhandled and beaten at the time of arrest. Twenty-five out of forty-five children whom we interviewed and who were arrested, said they had been beaten by police at the time of arrest and/or at the police station. Seven out of the forty-five said they had not been beaten. Once arrested, street children are held under deplorable physical conditions in crowded police station cells, often without toilets or bedding, with little food, and inadequate supplies of water. They are almost always mixed with adults, beaten and harassed by police in the station, and held for periods extending from several days to weeks without any review of the legality of their detention by judicial authorities. One child reported being held in a police lockup for two months without being charged with an offense and without any review of the legality of the detention before he was finally released by police, despite Kenyan

---

and Working Children, p. 15.

legal requirements that a person arrested without a warrant be brought before a magistrate without delay, and ordinarily within twenty-four hours.

Once arrested, children may have their cases referred by police to court for processing. Children's cases are supposed to be heard in special juvenile courts, established under the Children and Young Persons Act.[3] The jurisdiction of juvenile courts extends to both criminal matters and to non-criminal "protection or discipline" matters—essentially status offenses. Status offenses are acts that would not be offenses if committed by an adult; for example, truancy, running away from home, or being "incorrigible." Under Article 21 of the Children and Young Persons Act, children who are "in need of protection or discipline" are children under the age of sixteen who are deserted, parentless, beggars, vagrants, "uncontrollable," or who fall into "bad associations." "Protection or discipline" cases and criminal cases are treated very similarly, and the categorizations are thus in many ways arbitrary and meaningless. For example, a fifteen-year-old street boy who is arrested by police on "vagrancy" grounds could be treated as either a criminal case or a "protection or discipline" case, depending on the discretion of the magistrate; either way, the boy could be finally committed by court to an approved school.

Despite the requirement that children's cases be heard in special juvenile courts, we found that children's cases are often heard in regular courts along with adult cases, where children are tried without the special protections accorded to juveniles under Kenyan law. However, even when their cases are heard in juvenile court, the proceedings are rushed and do not allow children fair opportunities to be heard. To our knowledge, none of the children we interviewed were ever represented by legal or other counsel in either juvenile or regular courts, and only a few said that a parent or guardian was present at the proceedings. Confused and frightened in court, children often do not understand the nature of the legal proceedings or the dispositions of their cases. Some said they were advised by cell mates, and in one case even by the magistrate, to plead guilty to crimes, including the crime of vagrancy, in order to avoid otherwise lengthy periods of detention in remand institutions.

Pending final adjudication and disposition of their cases, street children are committed by courts to temporary detention in remand institutions— to juvenile remand homes (for children fifteen years old and younger) or to adult remand prisons (for children at least fourteen years old) where they may languish for indefinite periods of time, usually between several weeks and several months, before a final disposition is reached on their cases. There are no limits under

---

[3] Chapter 141 of the Laws of Kenya.

Kenyan law on the amount of time that a person can be detained in a remand institution. Although remand homes are meant to be only temporary holding centers for children, we found that some children had spent several years in remand homes pending adjudication of their cases—without any education or recreational activities at all to provide them with stimulation.

Conditions in remand were particularly disturbing in adult remand prisons, where children as young as fourteen may be held. Rooms were so crowded that children reported sleeping sitting up or next to toilets because there was not enough room elsewhere. Boys said they endured extreme physical abuse, usually by older inmates and sometimes by prison guards. Sexual harassment by inmates was also reported, along with failure of guards to protect children from inmate abuse. As mentioned above, the notoriety of remand centers, with regard to both the conditions within and the limitless duration of remand periods, leads some children to plead guilty to offenses they have not committed in order to avoid remand altogether.

From remand, children may be finally committed by courts to approved schools (if the child is fifteen years old or younger), borstal institutions (for boys at least fifteen years old) and adult prisons (if the child is at least fourteen years old). A wide range of alternatives to custodial treatment are provided for under the Children and Young Persons Act, yet magistrates still tend to overuse institutionalization as a remedial measure for street children. Conditions in these institutions fail to provide children with the education and rehabilitative training that they purport to, and children leave these institutions emotionally and physically scarred, stigmatized, and negatively influenced by their peers who may be serious criminal offenders. Little effort is made to separate the children by category of their underlying offense or status, resulting in children who are homeless being mixed with children convicted of serious criminal offenses. Further, many children complained about the infliction of corporal punishment by staff, and physical abuse by other boys. In approved schools, canings, deprivation of home leave, and labor are used as punishments. Punishments in borstal institutions (for boys) were found to be particularly cruel—boys reported the use of hard labor (digging), solitary confinement in dark and wet isolation rooms, reductions in diet, and public floggings.

The treatment of street children by police, the procedures by which children are confined to correctional institutions, and the conditions in these institutions will be discussed in this report. The Kenyan government is failing to adequately address the social and economic hardships which lead children to the streets. Moreover, its system of correctional institutions fails to provide children with the rehabilitation, support, and education required to assist them to become responsible and capable members of society. The complex and outdated legal provisions and enforcement mechanisms which currently exist in Kenya result in the criminalization and mistreatment of street children. Although the Kenyan government is currently in the process of considering much needed amendment of a number of laws relevant to street children, including the Children and Young Persons Act, it is feared that little real change will come about. Human Rights Watch hopes that this report may be useful in identifying some of the specific areas in need of reform, in the interest of improving the lives of street children in Kenya.

Recommendations

Human Rights Watch makes the following recommendations concerning the treatment of street children by police and in the juvenile justice system:

To the Kenyan Government:
- The government should promptly submit its overdue report on Kenya's compliance with the U.N. Convention on the Rights of the Child to the Committee on the Rights of the Child.

- The government should promptly sign and ratify the African Charter on the Rights and Welfare of the Child.

To the Attorney General*:*
- As a matter of priority, the attorney general should complete the redrafting of the Children Bill and other relevant laws requiring reform, in close consultation and cooperation with the Kenyan NGO community. We urge the attorney general to take into account the recommendations below in redrafting the Children Bill and other laws.

- The attorney general should seek the technical assistance of the U.N. Crime Prevention and Criminal Justice Division towards the reform of laws relating to juvenile justice.

- The Births and Death Registration Act (Chapter 149 of the Laws of Kenya) should be amended to ensure that all births in Kenya are duly recorded and registered so that children and their families know their age.

- The Police Act (Chapter 85 of the Laws of Kenya) should be amended to include clear guidelines on the use of force by police. The Police Act currently contains guidelines on the use of firearms only.

- The Vagrancy Act (Chapter 58 of the Laws of Kenya) should be repealed or amended so that "having no fixed abode," "begging," or having neither "lawful employment nor lawful means of subsistence" are no longer criminal offenses for street children and not grounds for arrest.

- The Children and Young Persons Act should be amended accordingly:

    Article 6, which allows police to detain sixteen and seventeen-year-old children with adults, should be amended so that children—those under eighteen—are never detained with adults.

    Article 11 should be amended to place a time limit on the period that children can be detained on remand pending adjudication of their cases, and to prohibit remanding children to adult remand prisons.

    Article 12 should be amended so that children who are accused jointly with adults of criminal offenses are tried in juvenile courts.

    Article 17 should be amended so that corporal punishment is never used as a correctional measure.

    Article 17 should be amended so that children are never committed to adult prisons.

    Article 46 should be amended to prohibit the transfer of children from an approved school to a borstal institution or prison, and to prohibit the prolonging of a child's sentence in an approved school.

- The Borstal Institutions Act (Chapter 93 of the Laws of Kenya) should be amended to:
    Eliminate the following disciplinary practices in borstal institutions:
        corporal punishment (Article 33.5);
        solitary confinement (Articles 32, 33.5); and
        reduction in diet (Articles 32, 33.5).
    Prohibit the transfer of children from a borstal to prison (Article 42).

- The right of children to maintain contacts with the outside world through uncensored correspondence and visitations should be respected. The Borstal Institutions Rules (subsidiary legislation under Article 52 of the Borstal Institutions Act) should be amended to eliminate the censorship of children's correspondence (Rule 45) and to eliminate the use of deprivation of the right to write and receive correspondence as punishment (Rule 42).

Regarding the Police:

- The Kenyan government should reiterate the absolute prohibition on physical abuse of children by police, and should prosecute any police officer found guilty of such abuse to the full extent of the law.

- Prompt investigations of complaints concerning police mistreatment of children should be conducted, their findings made public, and disciplinary measures and criminal proceedings ordered where appropriate.

- The attorney general should establish a special independent commission for the receipt of complaints concerning police mistreatment of street children (having special cognizance of the use of deadly force, custodial abuse, sexual abuse, and extortion). The commission should be directly accessible to street children and should be equipped and empowered to subpoena witnesses, conduct investigations, and to bring complaints to the Attorney General's Office and the Criminal Investigation Department.

- Police should be specially educated and trained on how to handle cases of street children with a view towards sensitizing police to the special needs of children and ensuring that rights accorded to children, under international and Kenyan law, are enforced.

- Measures should be taken to ensure that children are not detained beyond the permissible periods under law; the validity of any detention extending beyond twenty-four hours should be promptly reviewed by judicial authorities or the child should be released.

- Police should make diligent and systematic efforts to determine the age of young persons they arrest, to ensure that children are identified and dealt with as children. If necessary to refer children's cases to court, cases should be referred to juvenile court.

Regarding the Juvenile Courts:
- Resources should be directed towards the establishment of specialized juvenile courts in Kenya for the handling of children's cases. Currently, only one specialized juvenile court exists in all of Kenya, in Nairobi.

- Magistrates should make diligent and systematic efforts to determine the age of young persons appearing before them to ensure that children are identified and treated as children, in juvenile courts according to law.

- Magistrates who handle juvenile cases should be specially educated and trained on how to handle children's cases, with a view towards sensitizing the judiciary to the special needs of children and ensuring that the rights accorded to children, under both international and Kenyan law, are enforced.

- The government should take steps to provide children in court with free legal and other assistance in their cases. Magistrates should make special efforts to ensure that children understand the nature of the proceedings and the status and disposition of their cases. Parents or family members should take part in the proceedings.

- The Ministry of Home Affairs should ease restrictions on the procedures for becoming an approved officer (an officer approved by the government to work on issues related to the protection and care of children, including appearing on behalf of children in juvenile court). NGO representatives who work with street children should be allowed to act as approved officers and to provide assistance to street children in juvenile court.

- Magistrates should always consider social inquiry reports by children's officers or probation officers before ordering the deprivation of a child's liberty.

- Alternatives to institutionalization should be given the highest priority in determining correctional measures.

- All efforts should be made to reunite children with their families, or to place them in appropriate children's homes, approved voluntary institutions, and NGO-run programs for street children.

- The deprivation of liberty in a correctional institution (approved school, borstal institution, or prison) should only be ordered as a last resort and for the shortest period necessary.

- Children who are "in need of protection or discipline" should not be committed to the same institutions as children who are convicted of criminal offenses.

- Court practice should be changed, so that cases of children who are "in need of protection or discipline" are not treated as criminal cases.

Regarding Remand Institutions, Approved Schools, and Borstal Institutions:

- The Children's Department should undertake measures to ensure that children are separated according to the nature of their underlying offenses or status, and separated in detention or correctional facilities accordingly.

- Every juvenile confined in a detention or correctional facility should have immediate access to adequate medical care and medical facilities for the prevention and treatment of illness. Every juvenile in custodial care who is ill, who complains of illness or who demonstrates symptoms of illness, physical or mental, should be examined promptly by a qualified medical officer and treated.

- Corporal punishment and physical abuse by staff against children should be strictly prohibited. Staff found to have abused children should be appropriately disciplined, including by dismissal. Where appropriate, criminal charges should be brought against the staff.

- The practice of suspending home leave to children confined in approved schools, as punishment, should be ended.

- The use of corporal punishment in approved schools (as authorized in the Internal Regulations of the Children's Department) should be discontinued.

- The Children's Department and the Prisons Department should ensure that children are provided with effective mechanisms to make uncensored complaints about the conduct of institutional staff members or the conditions of confinement.

Regarding Education:
- The government should undertake measures to provide free primary level education to street children in Kenya, and to provide for the associated costs of education (books, uniforms, and "building fund" contributions or "school fees") for such children.

- The government should establish a special fund for the provision of the associated costs of primary level education to children from low-income families throughout Kenya, for whom the payment of book, uniforms, and "school fees" are prohibitive. Women, as heads of single parent households, and others who care for children and are unable to afford the associated costs of primary education should be encouraged to apply for support to enable children to stay in school.

- The Prisons Department should ensure that borstal institutions provide primary level education for all boys, not just for boys in standards 7 and 8.

- The Children's Department should ensure that girls committed to approved schools are provided with equal access to opportunities for secondary level education. Currently only boys have the opportunity of continuing their education beyond the primary level in approved schools.

To the United Nations:
- The U.N. Special Rapporteur on Torture and Other Forms of Cruel, Inhuman or Degrading Treatment or Punishment should visit Kenya and investigate police abuse of street children, and abuse of children in borstal institutions and adult remand prisons.

- The U.N. Working Group on Arbitrary Detention should visit Kenya and investigate the detention of children in police station lockups, juvenile remand homes and adult remand prisons.

- The U.N. Committee on the Rights of the Child should devote one of its theme days to police violence against street children.

To Donor Country Governments:
- Aid should be earmarked for the training of police and law enforcement personnel on the rights of the child and on the handling of juvenile cases.

- Aid should be earmarked for the creation of specialized courts for children (juvenile courts or family courts), and for the training of magistrates on the rights of the child and on the handling of juvenile cases.

- Aid should be earmarked to facilitate the reunification of street children with their families.

- Realizing that deprivation of liberty should be ordered only as a last resort for children, aid should be earmarked to improve conditions in remand institutions, approved schools, and borstal institutions to provide for the health, physical, educational and recreational needs of children committed there.

- Aid should be earmarked for the purposes of defraying the associated costs of primary school attendance, such as book fees, uniforms, and building maintenance costs, which families currently must provide.

- Donor country governments should use their influence with the Kenyan government to seek accountability of law enforcement personnel, prison officers, and correctional school officers for abuses committed against street children, including extortion, physical abuse and sexual abuse.

- Donor country governments should use their influence to press the attorney general for meaningful reform of existing legislation affecting children, to bring legislation into compliance with the Convention on the Rights of the Child—in the drafting of the revised Children Bill and other legislation.

To NGOs:
- NGOs should maintain detailed records of incidents of violence between police and children in order to monitor and document abuses by police. They should submit these records to the government-created Standing Committee on Human Rights, and coordinate with other NGOs active in the protection of human rights to strengthen NGO efforts in this area.

II. BACKGROUND

I was schooled up to standard 3. I was chased away from the school because I couldn't pay the school fees, and I didn't have a uniform. Then I was home for a while, with my mother and brothers and sisters, and I started hanging out on the streets. That's how I came to be a street boy.[4]

The Growing Presence of Street Children

Before discussing the treatment of street children within the juvenile justice system, it is important to address the complex factors that contribute to the "phenomenon" of street children in Kenya. In addition to deep rooted and complex socio-economic factors, direct government actions have also contributed to the mounting presence of street children in Kenya.

Between 1980 and 1990 the urban population in Kenya doubled, with most of the growth concentrated in Nairobi, the capital, and Mombasa, the second largest city.[5] Migration from rural areas to urban centers increased dramatically with poor families being driven from their homes by landlessness, drought and unemployment. A sprawling collection of slum settlements spread over the outskirts of Nairobi, including the areas of Mathare Valley, Huruma, Dandore, Kariobangi, Kibera, Korogocho and Ngara. With thousands of new urban slum dwellers, including a large number of single-parent households headed by women,[6] the numbers of children[7] living on the streets began to rise dramatically. The

---

[4] Human Rights Watch interview with Tom, Kisumu, September 22, 1996. The names of children we interviewed have been changed for their protection.

[5] Dorothy Munyakho, *Kenya: Child newcomers in the urban jungle* (UNICEF Innocenti Studies, 1992), p. 3.

[6] Nearly one-third of Kenyan households are headed by women. In low-income areas the proportion is even higher. In the Mathare slum area of Nairobi, between 60 and 80 percent of all households are headed by women. In UNICEF's 1992 "Situation Analysis of Children and Women in Kenya," female headship of a family is argued to be one of the factors most closely associated with poverty. Ibid., p. 10.

[7] In this report, the word "children" refers to anyone under the age of eighteen. The U.N. Convention on the Rights of the Child, ratified by Kenya in 1990, defines a child as "every human being below the age of eighteen years unless, under the law applicable to

Background

annual growth rate of the street children population was put at 10 percent in 1993.[8] There are currently estimated to be 25,000 street children in Nairobi alone and upwards of 40,000 nationwide,[9] compared to an estimated 3,600 in Nairobi and 16,300 nationwide in 1989.[10] A study on street children initiated by the Attorney General's Office in 1989, and completed in 1991, concluded that Kenya was sitting on a "time bomb."[11]

Numerous and complex socio-economic factors have fueled the rising presence of children on the streets. Views expressed in a 1993 UNICEF International Child Development Center report point towards the increasingly difficult circumstances of women, as heads of single-parent households, as a major contributing factor. Like in many places in the world, Kenyan women have had comparatively less access to education and paid employment opportunities than men and are less represented in higher-paying occupations. Yet, overwhelmingly, it is the women who take responsibility for raising their children in single-parent households. The single-parent phenomenon "is the result of a combination of social and economic factors, including the increasing employment of women outside the home, connected to the impact of rapid urbanization and the unfamiliar

---

the child, majority is attained earlier" (Article 1). U.N. Convention on the Rights of the Child, G.A. res. 44/25, annex 44 U.N. GAOR Supp. (No. 49) at 167, U.N. Doc. A/4/49 (1989) (entered into force September 2, 1990). Relevant sections of the text of the Convention on the Rights of the Child are set forth in Appendix A.

[8] Kenya Law Reform Commission, "A New Law on Children: Report of the Child Law Task Force," February 1993 ("Report of the Child Law Task Force"), Section 3.16, p. 33.

[9] Human Rights Watch interview with Josephine Mulli, Idah Mutinde, and Macharia Komo, Undugu Society of Kenya, Nairobi, September 18, 1996 ("Interview with Undugu Society"); Human Rights Watch interview with Kimaru Wakaruru, Executive Director, Child Welfare Society of Kenya, Nairobi, September 19, 1996 ("Interview with Child Welfare Society").

[10] Munyakho, *Kenya: Child newcomers in the urban jungle*, p. 3.

[11] Speech by Dr. Philista Onyango, Chairperson, ANPPCAN Regional Office, contained in ANPPCAN, *Hearing on Street Children in Kenya, Report on a hearing held in Nairobi on November 4-5, 1994* (Nairobi: ANPPCAN, 1995), p. 6.

city lifestyle on family ties and conjugal life."[12] Industrialization and urbanization have contributed to the breakdown of the traditional African extended family network which previously provided a safety net of support. Industrialization and urbanization have also contributed to a rise in cohabitation before or instead of marriage, leading to complications regarding the custody and support of children and the inheritance of property when the relationship ends. The Affiliation Act guaranteed that children born out of wedlock were entitled to financial support by the father until 1969, when it was repealed in parliament, with male parliamentarians arguing that the Act was being abused by women to claim support from more than one man for one child. Formal marriages are also becoming less stable, with divorce and separation rates on the rise. With the pressures of urban life and the breakdown of traditional support structures of the African extended family, women and their children are finding themselves increasingly at risk.[13]

The rising costs of education, coupled with these socio-economic factors, have further contributed to the increase of children on the streets. Kenya follows the "8-4-4" system: there are eight years of primary level education, standards 1-8, followed by forms 1-4 of secondary level education, followed by four years of university level education. When the Kenyan government ratified the International Covenant on Economic, Social and Cultural Rights in 1976, it recognized "the right of everyone to education," and that with a view towards achieving progressively the full realization of this right, "primary education shall be compulsory and free to all."[14] The Convention on the Rights of the Child, ratified by Kenya in 1990, provides for the same.[15] Although not yet compulsory, primary level education (standards 1-8) in Kenya is tuition-free.[16] As early as 1961 the Kenya African

---

[12] Ibid., p. 11.

[13] Ibid., pp. 11-13.

[14] International Covenant on Economic, Social and Cultural Rights, G.A. Res. 2200 (XXI), 21 U.N. GAOR Supp. (No. 16), U.N. Doc. A/6316 (entered into force January 3, 1976), Article 13.

[15] Convention on the Rights of the Child, Article 28. The African Charter on the Rights and Welfare of the Child (not yet ratified by Kenya, and not yet entered into force) similarly recognizes the right to education for all children in Article 11, and that with a view towards achieving the full realization of that right, states parties shall "provide free and compulsory basic education."

[16] Secondary level education and higher education are not tuition-free.

National Union (KANU), which has been in charge of government since 1963, committed itself to providing free primary level education for every child.[17] Hoewever, in practice not all children have been able to benefit from the plan for free primary education. Dropout rates are high, even at the primary school level, in large part because of the heavy expenses incurred by families to finance their children's primary education. Between 40 and 60 percent of children living in the slum areas of Nairobi, Kisumu and Mombasa do not attend primary school, compared to enrollment rates of about 80 percent in the urban population as a whole.[18] The reality is that education in Kenya, even at the primary level, is not free.

While there are no tuition fees for primary education, parents must provide for the costs of textbooks, uniforms, stationery, and building and maintaining schools, by making "voluntary" contributions to the "development fund" or "building fund." The government pays for teachers' salaries and some school equipment and some textbooks.[19] This cost-sharing arrangement between the government and parents is simply beyond the means of many families from which street children come. Indeed, many street children who we interviewed said they had taken to the streets after being thrown out of school for not being able to pay school fees or because they did not have uniforms or shoes.[20]

---

[17] George S. Eshiwani, *Education in Kenya Since Independence* (Nairobi: East African Educational Publishers, 1993), pp. 138-39. Secondary school education is more expensive. In addition to other related costs, as families must pay tuition fees as well as other costs.

[18] Munyakho, *Kenya: Child newcomers in the urban jungle*, p. 20.

[19] Eshiwani, *Education in Kenya Since Independence*, pp. 138-39.

[20] Nairobi city education authorities and NGOs have responded to this crisis in education by running "non-formal" schools for children that do away with many of the requirements which place formal education beyond the reach of urban slum-dwellers, such as uniforms, shoes, the requirement of a birth certificate for admission, and age-limits for admission to standard 1. School fees are lower and may be paid in monthly installments instead of in lump sums each semester. The curriculums in the schools vary, with some schools catering to working children, some schools emphasizing vocational and survival skills, and others attempting to follow the national syllabus and enrolling children for national exams following completion of standard 8 (the KCPE exam). The number of these "non-formal" schools are few, however, and are still beyond the reach of many children. Non-formal schools are concentrated in urban areas, and while a large number of street

Large scale slum clearance operations undertaken by city authorities have been another factor contributing to the rise of street children. With policies ostensibly aimed at maintaining Kenyan cities at the highest standards of hygiene, the government uses urban planning restrictions, which forbid the development of squatter settlements, to remove residents with the eviction and destruction of their homes—leaving already marginalized slum dwellers and their families homeless. These operations are often undertaken without providing assistance, alternative arrangements, or notice to evicted residents, with families sometimes literally being uprooted from their homes and left to fend for themselves on the streets.

Finally, in recent years, state-sponsored ethnic violence in the west and Rift Valley of Kenya has also contributed to the internal displacement and migration of families, as well as the breakup of families.[21] In 1991, after the government was forced to concede to a multiparty system, the Moi government was responsible for instigating "ethnic" violence in order to punish those ethnic groups which supported the political opposition and to reward its own supporters with illegally obtained land. Although the large-scale attacks that characterized the violence have diminished since 1994, periodic incidents continue. Most of those displaced belong to the Kikuyu, Luo and Luhya ethnic groups and were attacked by members of the Kalenjin ethnic group (President Moi's group) as well as the Maasai. Retaliatory attacks did occur, but tended to be more random and opportunistic in character, and most of the displaced Kalenjin have since returned to their land. However, thousands others of the estimated 300,000 displaced have still not returned to their land because of government inaction to provide adequate security. The government has also been responsible for forcibly dispersing groups of displaced in order to avoid the attention of humanitarian and human rights groups and to evade its responsibility to return these people to their land and

---

children do come from urban slum settlements, others come from rural areas where "non-formal" schooling is largely unavailable and not an option.

[21] For an in-depth analysis of the "ethnic clashes" and subsequent government action against the displaced, see Human Rights Watch/Africa's report, *Divide and Rule: State Sponsored Ethnic Violence in Kenya* (New York: Human Rights Watch, 1993); Human Rights Watch/Africa, "Multipartyism Betrayed in Kenya: Continuing Rural Violence and Restrictions on Freedom of Speech and Assembly," *A Human Rights Watch Short Report*, vol. 6, no. 5, July 1994; Human Rights Watch/Africa, "Old Habits Die Hard: Rights Abuses Follow Renewed Foreign Aid Commitment," *A Human Rights Watch Short Report*, vol. 7, no. 6, July 1995; Human Rights Watch/Africa, *Failing the Internally Displaced: the UNDP Displaced Persons Program in Kenya* (New York: Human Rights Watch, 1997).

livelihood. Since most of those displaced by the "ethnic" violence were subsistence farmers with little formal education, they have been rendered virtually destitute. Many members of the internally displaced Kikuyu, Luo and Luhya ethnic groups have drifted to the urban slum areas.

The United Nations has estimated that as much as 75 percent of the estimated 300,000 displaced were children.[22] A number of Kikuyu boys and girls whom we interviewed in Nairobi and in Mombasa said they were forced to flee from their homes and were separated from their families during "tribal clashes," as the violence is known, in the west and Rift Valley of Kenya in 1992 and 93. They had come to Nairobi in search of family members or simply because there was nowhere else for them to go:

> I had to flee in the middle of the night. I woke up and our house was on fire. There was no one left in the house, and I just ran. I stayed in a camp for about a year with a lot of other people who had to flee like me. After a while, people started talking about going back to their homes. I went back to my home [in Molo, in the Rift Valley], but our home was not there and my family was gone. The neighbors said they had heard nothing about my parents. So I came to Nairobi to look for my uncle and found him. He was surprised to see me—he said he thought we had all been killed. But he couldn't keep me with him. Sometimes I still see him when I can, but he can't take care of me.[23]

Another Kikuyu boy said, "we're not real street boys, we were forced to leave our homes during the clashes. I had to run out of the house and hide at night—our house was burning. I came back the next day and my parents and brothers and sisters were gone. I don't know where they went. I came to Nairobi, and haven't been back [to Molo] since."[24]

---

[22] John Rogge, "The Internally Displaced Population in Nyanza, Western and Rift Valley Province: A Needs Assessment and a Program Proposal for Rehabilitation," United Nations Development Program, September 1993, Part 3 (3.8).

[23] Human Rights Watch interview with David, Nairobi, September 24, 1996.

[24] Human Rights Watch interview with Simon, Nairobi, September 26, 1996.

Whatever the causes are, the numbers of children living on the street are expected to continue to rise. In addition to addressing the deep rooted and complex factors which contribute to their existence on the streets, the Kenyan government must take steps to address the treatment of street children by law enforcement and within the juvenile justice system, and by Kenyan society as a whole.

III. POLICE ABUSES AGAINST STREET CHILDREN

We usually carry sacks (for garbage picking). The [Kisumu] police beat us up and put us in our sacks. Even if we're just walking around, doing nothing. If you don't give them money, they take you to the station. Usually they ask us questions about thefts that have happened. They search us. If we have money, they take it. If we don't have money, we have to talk to them really nicely, or else they'll take you to the police station.[25]

Life on the streets is dangerous enough for street children without their having to be on guard against police, the very people who are supposed to protect them. While we recognize that some police work to help street children and to reunite them with their families, many others do just the opposite, harassing and abusing the children and those who seek to help them. One street worker in Nairobi described being questioned by police: "they wanted to know who I am, and what business I have with the kids. I told them I am their friend and teacher. The police told me that I am doing zero work as those boys are criminals. . . . I convinced them that these boys can be rehabilitated if we use the right approach. They said it is not possible."[26]

Police tend to view street children as hardened criminals, who must be treated with severity. Police also abuse and exploit the children for their own personal gain. Children we interviewed said they were frequently harassed, beaten, and had their money taken from them by police on the streets. Girls in Nairobi reported being sexually propositioned or coerced into having sex with police. The level of abuse is rising to a dangerous level. In recent years, there have been alarming incidents of police use of lethal force against street children resulting in death. The Executive Director of the Undugu Society of Kenya has been cited as stating that "Kenya's dispossessed youngsters don't face the same level of public hostility as their counterparts in South America, but violence against the street kids

---

[25] Human Rights Watch interview with Wycliffe, Kisumu, September 22, 1996.

[26] NGO written response to Human Rights Watch questionnaire, March 27, 1997, anonymity requested.

has been increasing."[27] With their ranks growing, street children are likely to continue to suffer from such abuses unless immediate measures are taken to ensure better training and strict accountability of law enforcement personnel.

International and Kenyan Standards

The conduct of police regarding the use of force is prescribed under international law by the U.N. Code of Conduct for Law Enforcement Officials.[28] Law enforcement officials "shall respect and protect human dignity and maintain and uphold the human rights of all persons" in the performance of their duties (Article 2). The human rights that must be "protected, maintained and upheld" are those identified and protected by national and international law, including the International Covenant on Civil and Political Rights (ICCPR) which was ratified by Kenya in 1976.[29] Under Article 7 of the ICCPR, no one shall be subjected to torture or to cruel, inhuman or degrading treatment or punishment.[30] Under the Code of Conduct, no law enforcement official may inflict, instigate or tolerate such treatment or punishment against any person (Article 5).

Force may only be used as is reasonably necessary to prevent the commission of a crime or to effect a lawful arrest; no force may be used beyond

---

[27] Kirsty Scott, "Adrift on a tide of apathy," *The Herald* (Glasgow, Scotland), March 25, 1995.

[28] U.N. Code of Conduct for Law Enforcement Officials, G.A. Res. 34/169, annex, 34, U.N. GAOR Supp. (No. 46) at 186, U.N. Doc. A/34/46 (1979) ("Code of Conduct"). The Code of Conduct is not a treaty, and therefore its provisions are not binding. However, it does constitute authoritative interpretation and explanation of accepted standards that are binding, either because they are found in treaty law or because they are part of customary international law. The full text of the Code of Conduct is set forth in Appendix D.

[29] Code of Conduct, commentary to Article 2. *See also* U.N. Basic Principles on the Use of Force and Firearms by Law Enforcement Officials, Eighth United Nations Congress on the Prevention of Crime and the Treatment of Offenders, Havana, 27 August to 7 September 1990, U.N. Doc. A/CONF.144/28/Rev.1 at 112 (1990) ("Basic Principles"). The full text of the Basic Principles is set forth in Appendix E.

[30] International Covenant on Civil and Political Rights, G.A. Res. 2200 (XXI), 21 U.N. GAOR Supp. (No. 16), U.N. Doc. A/6316 (entered into force January 3, 1976).

that which is reasonably necessary to effect that purpose.[31] The Kenyan Police Act contains no guidelines on the use of force, aside from the use of firearms, by police. However, police regulations contained in the Police Act recognize an officer's unlawful use of violence or the unlawful striking of a person as a disciplinary offense.[32] We strongly recommend that the Police Act be amended to include clear guidelines on the limits of use of general force that comply with the Code of Conduct and with the U.N. Basic Principles on the Use of Force and Firearms by Law Enforcement Officials.

With regard to the use of firearms, Article 28 of the Kenyan Police Act authorizes its use against "any person who by force attempts to prevent the lawful arrest of himself or of any other person." The officer must also have "reasonable ground to believe that he or any other person is in danger of grievous bodily harm or that he cannot otherwise . . . effect the arrest." Similarly, international standards provide that use of firearms should be avoided, especially against children, except when a suspected offender offers armed resistance or jeopardizes the lives of others, and less extreme measures cannot restrain him.[33] In cases where the lawful use of force and firearms is unavoidable, law enforcement officials must act with restraint in such use of force and in proportion to the seriousness of the offence and the legitimate objective to be achieved, with a view towards minimizing injury and preserving human life.[34]

Police Abuse of Children on the Streets

Categories of Law Enforcement Personnel

Street children in Kenya come into frequent contact with several different categories of law enforcement personnel: regular police, police reservists, administration police, and city *askaris* (the Kiswahili word for guard or soldier). In addition to regular police, the Kenyan Police Act provides for the establishment of the Kenyan Police Reserve, staffed by reserve officers (known as reservists) who

---

[31] Code of Conduct, commentary to Article 3.

[32] Police Regulations, Article 3(17). Police Regulations are established pursuant to Article 65 of the Police Act.

[33] *See* Code of Conduct, Article 3 and commentary; *see also* Basic Principles, Article 9.

[34] *See* Code of Conduct, commentary to Article 3; Basic Principles, Article 5.

are employed on a part-time basis to perform regular police duties.[35] As with regular police, reservists may be in uniform or plain clothes and may be armed.[36] As with regular police, they may be disciplined or prosecuted for their conduct under the Police Act or under any other law.[37] There are also armed and uniformed administration police appointed by the provincial administration who have duties and powers identical to those of ordinary police in conducting arrests.[38] Administration police are frequently associated with land and housing eviction operations, and are most active in rural areas. Several children we interviewed stated that administration police sometimes work together with regular police and reservists to round up street children. Finally, there are also unarmed and plainclothes city police, known as city *askaris*, who enforce city by-laws and are under the administration of a city commission (city council). City *askaris* sometimes work with administration police in slum clearance operations, and carry out arrests of street hawkers and vendors, including street children.[39]

It should be noted that children usually were unable to identify the particular law enforcement agency of the officers they spoke about, but simply referred to them as police or *askari*. As many are often in plain clothes, and none wear visible identification badges or name tags, children were generally unable to identify police by name. In the testimonies which follow, we have used the

---

[35] Human Rights Watch interview with Assistant Commissioner of Police Rhoda Kimundi, officer in charge of police prosecutions, Nairobi, 10/3/96 (Interview with the Assistant Commissioner of Police). *See also*, Police Act, Articles 52-58.

[36] Interview with the Assistant Commissioner of Police.

[37] Article 62 of the Police Act states that nothing in the act shall exempt police from legal proceedings, under any other laws in force, for an act constituting an offense under the Police Act, provided that no police officer shall be punished twice for the same offence. Article 58 provides that reservists who perform or purport to perform any police duties shall be subject to the same disciplinary provisions as regular police.

[38] H.B. Ndoria Gichery and Kabuya Miano, *The Constitution and Government of Kenya* (India: Sterling Publishers, 1987), p. 392. *See also* Administration Police Act, Chapter 85 of the Laws of Kenya, Article 13.

[39] Human Rights Watch interview with Njuguna Mutahi, Kenya Human Rights Commission, Nairobi, October 4, 1996 ("Interview with Kenya Human Rights Commission").

Physical Abuse on the Streets

Street children interviewed by Human Rights Watch recounted numerous incidents of physical abuse and harassment by police on the street. "We usually run away when we see the police because we know what will follow," said fourteen-year-old John about life on the streets in Nairobi.[40] Another Nairobi street boy told us that police harassment is constant, and that he had been beaten by police many times, the most recent time being just one day earlier in Westlands, Nairobi: "I was slapped around yesterday morning. The police just pounced on me while I was walking and started hitting me."[41] Children said they are frequently kicked, slapped, or hit with rifle butts for no reason other than the fact that they are street children. This type of treatment is not restricted to police in the Nairobi area, but was also reported in Kisumu.

In Mombasa children reported better treatment on the streets by police. Sixteen-year-old Peter, who had formerly lived on the streets in Nairobi, commented that "the police in Mombasa are better than in Nairobi. In Nairobi, even if you're just walking around doing nothing, the police might come and just pick you from the street and beat you up, and take you to the station. At least they don't do that here in Mombasa."[42] Another Mombasa street boy offered further explanation, "the police might not beat you, they just treat you like you're a sack, like you're not a person—they didn't beat me, but they threw me around and into the police vehicle like I was a sack."[43]

NGO street workers and many children told us that physical abuse by police is worse at night, when fewer people are on the streets and the risk of public censure is likely to be less. Roundups of street children usually happen at night, during the course of which children are often manhandled and beaten. Once detained, children are often further beaten at police stations, during interrogations and in lockups. This will be discussed in greater detail in Section IV (on confinement of children in police station lockups).

---

[40] Human Rights Watch interview with John, Nairobi, September 17, 1996.

[41] Human Rights Watch interview with Samuel, Nairobi, September 17, 1996.

[42] Human Rights Watch interview with Peter, Mombasa, September 28, 1996.

[43] Human Rights Watch interview with Jack, Mombasa, September 28, 1996.

Extortion

Aside from physical abuse, street children are also subject to extortion by police on the streets. They often must give up whatever meager amounts they have on their bodies to avoid arrest. In all three cities visited, children described having to pay money to police in order to avoid being taken into custody. "The policeman will say, 'now won't you give me some money for my tea,[44] and then I'll let you go'," said Helen, from the Mathare slum of Nairobi. Two weeks earlier, she had to give 500 shillings (approximately U.S.$10) to a policeman from Central Police Station in Nairobi in order to avoid arrest.[45] Fourteen-year-old Judy told us how she had been caught with several other girls near the 680 Hotel in Nairobi by plainclothes police, who asked her if she had any money. When she said she had no money, she was slapped and taken to Central Police Station, and then to court where she was charged with vagrancy.[46]

A social worker who works with street boys in Mombasa told us it is well known that police can be paid off to avoid arrest, but that street children rarely have the cash to do so;[47] fifteen-year-old Victoria told us, "I've never bribed the police. That's why I've been to jail ten times."[48]

Another street worker who works with children in Nairobi noted that "blackmailing" also occurs "when drugs are around" or "when the boys play *karata* (a gambling game)." He added that children who are arrested and brought to police stations are released immediately if they are able to pay money. "When they do not have money they sometimes stay two to three days in the police station and are subsequently released," he said.[49]

---

[44] The Kiswahili word for tea, *chai*, is widely used to refer to a bribe. It is not uncommon to be asked to give "something for chai" in Kenya.

[45] Human Rights Watch interview with Helen, Nairobi, September 29, 1996.

[46] Human Rights Watch interview with Judy, Nairobi, September 29, 1996.

[47] Human Rights Watch interview with social worker, Mombasa, September 29, 1996, anonymity requested.

[48] Human Rights Watch interview with Victoria, Nairobi, October 2, 1996.

[49] NGO written response to Human Rights Watch questionnaire, March 27, 1997, anonymity requested.

Sexual Abuse of Street Girls

Even more disturbing were the accounts of the sexual abuse of girls on Nairobi streets. In addition to money, street girls told us that they are asked for sex to avoid arrest or to be released from police custody. "When the police catch you, they ask you for money, or for sex, or else they'll take you to the police station," said Helen, who sleeps near City Market at night.[50] Five out of nine girls we interviewed on the streets of Nairobi, said that police had detained them and offered to release them in exchange for sex. The girls had been arrested on grounds of "loitering with intent to solicit" or vagrancy.

Sixteen-year-old Elizabeth, pregnant with her second child, described being arrested and locked in a cell in Central Police Station in Nairobi. She said that while her cell mates were asleep at night, two police men approached her and told her they would release her if she agreed to have sex with them. She said she refused, for which they punished her the next day by whipping her with a strip from an old rubber tire and ordering her to wash out the toilets. Elizabeth was eventually sentenced in City Court to two weeks in Langata Prison (for women) for "loitering with intent to solicit." Soon after her release from prison, she told us she was caught by police again, near Uhuru Park at night, and was put in a car where she was asked to have sex with one of the officers. "They didn't threaten me, but I was afraid, so I agreed to do it. I only had to have sex with that one policeman," she said.[51]

Eighteen-year-old Pamela, from Nyeri district in Central Province, recounted how she had been raped by a police man a year earlier:

> The police are always calling us names, threatening us, saying we're whores, trash, homeless, and beating us. Sexual abuse happens too. It happened to me once, here in Jeevanji [Gardens, a public park]. Four policemen came and arrested me near City Market. They started taking me to the Central Police Station, and brought me here to the park. One of them hit me and I fell down, and he came down on top of me. Another held me down while the policeman raped me. After he raped me, they walked me over to Central Police Station, and just let me go."[52]

---

[50] Human Rights Watch interview with Helen, Nairobi, September 29, 1996.

[51] Human Rights Watch interview with Elizabeth, Nairobi, October 2, 1996.

[52] Human Rights Watch interview with Pamela, Nairobi, September 24, 1996.

Pamela said she still sees the policeman who raped her patrolling the streets. She never complained to anyone about the rape. "Who would I complain to? If you go to the police to say anything, they'll either make you leave or they'll lock you up," she said.

Use of Deadly Force

Given the brutal attitude that many police display toward street children, it is not surprising to find that police violence against street children has occasionally risen to a deadly level in recent years. On August 11, 1994, a fifteen-year-old street boy named Simon Kamande Kampaniu was allegedly shot several times at close range and killed by police reservist Arvinderjit Singh Chadha in the Ngara area of Nairobi.[53] Public outrage mounted when it became known that the same reservist had been involved in the shooting and killing of five other street boys less than two months earlier on June 22, 1994. The reservist was eventually charged with the murder of Simon Kamande Kampaniu but was acquitted after trial in March 1995.

Presiding over the High Court in Nairobi, where the reservist was tried, Judge Samuel Bosire found that there was insufficient evidence to prove that the reservist had committed murder, or even the lesser charge of manslaughter.[54] The reservist admitted shooting Kampaniu and said that the boy was the eighth person he had killed in two years of duty.[55] He claimed that he had acted in self-defense after Kampaniu allegedly threatened him with a knife. The judge found that there was insufficient evidence to support the reservist's claims that Kampaniu had been armed, but still ruled that Kampaniu "was killed in the course of arrest after having committed a crime."[56]

Street children interviewed immediately after the verdict stated that the decision set a dangerous precedent for them and that it encouraged police to use excessive force against street children. Sixteen-year-old Evans Nyagah said the

---

[53] *The Economic Review* (Nairobi, Kenya), issue no. 109, November 14-20, 1994, pp. 4-5.

[54] Othello Gruduah, "Urchins criticize court," *East African Standard* (Nairobi, Kenya), March 23, 1995, p. 7.

[55] Manoah Esipisu, "Judge acquits Kenyan cop of murdering street kid," Reuters World Service, March 6, 1995, BC Cycle.

[56] Ibid.

ruling signaled to police that they could shoot street children at any time and claim that children were stealing as justification for their conduct.[57]

Eighteen months after the acquittal, another street boy named Daudi Ismail, known as Kajunia, was allegedly shot and killed by a reservist in Uhuru Park in Nairobi on September 22, 1996. The shooting occurred during Human Rights Watch's visit to Kenya, and we were able to interview several of the boys who were present at the shooting. Eighteen-year-old Moses described to us what happened that Sunday afternoon in Uhuru Park:

> It was around 3 p.m. We were by the restaurant in Uhuru Park. They had given us food in exchange for throwing out their garbage and we had just sat down to eat. There was a big group of us boys. Kajunia and David went off to go to the bathroom. Some other boys went off to get water for us all to drink. Then we saw Paul, a police reservist, who we recognized right away—he usually carries a whip. He and his partner got out of their car, about fifty meters away, and started coming towards us. Paul was holding a whip in his left hand. We got up and started to run away. We were all running and shouting, and some of the smaller boys were caught and whipped. I jumped over a fence and crouched down low, near the Cathedral. David and Kajunia had gone down into a ditch which runs through a part of the park, and gone to the bathroom in a tunnel. David came out first and was able to get away in time. Kajunia was just coming out when Paul got him. Paul had his gun out and pointed into the ditch and fired. A few minutes later, he walked to his car and drove away. A crowd gathered around Kajunia's body, and the police came about fifteen minutes later. Us boys stood back a little at a distance. We were afraid to come too near. The police didn't come to us and ask any questions, except they asked one of the small boys what Kajunia's name was, that was all.[58]

We asked the boys present at the shooting whether Kajunia had attempted to steal a purse, as one newspaper article alleged, and whether Kajunia had been

---

[57] Othello Gruduah, "Urchins criticize court."

[58] Human Rights Watch interview with Moses, Nairobi, September 24, 1996.

armed.[59] David, who had been with Kajunia just before he was killed, responded angrily to that allegation:

> If Kajunia had stolen a purse, where was the purse? There was nothing next to his body, no purse, no weapon. He wasn't armed. If he had tried to steal a purse, then from who? There was no one accusing him of stealing. Even if they thought we were stealing, the police should have whipped him, not killed him."[60]

David added that Kajunia was shot at point blank range, that he had his arms raised in surrender when he was shot, and that the reservist spat on his body before he walked away.

Police Accountability

Establishing police accountability is seriously hampered by the fact that children must complain directly to police about police abuse. The threat of repercussions by police is a serious deterrent to any child coming forward to testify or make complaints against police. Several children told us that for them to even go near a police station would be risking jail time for them. Thus, the majority of cases of police abuse of street children go undetected and unreported. Nevertheless, boys who witnessed the shooting of Kajunia told us they would be willing to come forward if provided with legal protection: "We're afraid and we're nervous. We can't just go to the police station and tell them what happened. We would go if we had protection, if we had a lawyer behind us."[61]

According to Rhoda Kimundi, an assistant commissioner of police, the process of making a complaint against a police officer works as follows. There is no special disciplinary unit within the police for the registering of complaints against officers. Individuals can lodge their complaints at any police station. The senior-most officer there would then direct the complaint to another police station or to the police commissioner for investigation. "We don't spare anything on our

---

[59] "Street urchin shot dead by cop reservist," *East African Standard* (Nairobi, Kenya), September 24, 1996, p. 3.

[60] Human Rights Watch interview with David, Nairobi, September 24, 1996.

[61] Human Rights Watch interview with Moses, Nairobi, September 24, 1996.

officers. They can be sacked, depending on the seriousness of the complaint. They can even be prosecuted in court," she said.[62]

In practice, however, we found that although any individual can lodge a complaint with police at any station, "the police are not bound by law to act, which means that in cases where they are being criticized, it is most unlikely that any decisive action will be taken."[63] Thus even if a child were to muster up the courage and defiance to complain to police about police abuse, there is no guarantee that the complaint will be followed up or answered. With regard to legal redress, it is critical to note that police themselves are the ones who make the determination whether or not to level a criminal charge against an officer who is accused of violating the law. "The eminence of the police in the criminal trial process is emphasized by the fact that they must prepare the necessary charge sheet before a trial court can arbitrate over a matter of abuse."[64] In cases where police do decide to file a criminal charge sheet against another officer, the charge sheet is passed to a prosecutor who is a also a member of the police force. The bulk of criminal cases in Kenya are government prosecuted, by "police prosecutors" who are usually employed within a division of the police known as the Criminal Investigation Department (CID).[65] Police prosecutors are not attorneys but are trained to prosecute criminal cases. They often prosecute criminal cases against ordinary citizens, including street children, as well as cases against other police, raising the possibility of conflict of interest in the latter cases.[66] If the case is very serious, or if a senior or "high ranking" officer is involved, a state counsel from the Attorney General's Office prosecutes the case.[67]

---

[62] Interview with the Assistant Commissioner of Police.

[63] African Network for the Prevention and Protection Against Child Abuse and Neglect (ANPPCAN) Kenya's written response to Human Rights Watch questionnaire, March 11, 1997 ("ANPPCAN Kenya Response.")

[64] Ibid.

[65] Interview with the Assistant Commissioner of Police.

[66] State counsels, under the Attorney General's Office, prosecute only high level cases. According to Assistant Commissioner of Police Kimundi, state counsels would prosecute cases involving "very serious offenses" or high ranking senior police officers.

[67] Interview with the Assistant Commissioner of Police

The Kenya Human Rights Commission, an NGO, reported that police killed eighty-eight people in the first nine months of 1996. According to the Attorney General's Office, twelve police officers were charged with brutality and wrongful killings in 1996. The government prosecuted only several of these cases, resulting in two convictions for murder.[68]

Additionally, it is possible for an individual to bring a private criminal action against the police or an individual. However, this is extremely costly and is well beyond the means of street children and NGOs that seek to assist them :

> The government raised court fees for filing and hearing cases by several hundred percent in 1995. The daily rate for arguing a case before a judge, for example, rose from $10 to $50. The Law Society of Kenya and many attorneys strongly opposed the increase, saying that the new charges would deny the majority of citizens access to the courts.[69]

The difficulties in mounting a private criminal action against the police are large. This is especially true for street children, who are impoverished and live outside the protection of responsible adults. Further, the attorney general is authorized to take over and continue or discontinue any criminal action which is commenced by an individual.[70]

NGOs have assisted street children in filing preliminary complaints with the police about police misconduct,[71] but have not themselves commenced private legal actions against police, with the exception of Kituo Cha Sheria (an NGO which engages in legal advocacy on behalf of the poor). Even if children's NGOs had the legal and financial resources to do this, the obstacles which they face are high and costly. One NGO that was actively involved in bringing to light facts surrounding the shooting and killing of Simon Kampaniu Kamande was denied registration after it became involved in the case, and has since registered under a new name.

---

[68] U.S. Department of State, Kenya Country Report on Human Rights for 1996, Section 1(a).

[69] Ibid., Section 1(e).

[70] Constitution of Kenya, Article 26.

[71] The Kenya Alliance for the Advancement of Children reportedly plans to organize training for NGOs on how to file complaints against police.

Members of that NGO have reportedly been harassed and one member was subjected to short-term arrest by police. Police often view NGOs that work with street children with suspicion and disdain, and NGOs are wary of antagonizing police and jeopardizing their ability to work with the children.

Evidence of the impunity of police is reflected in the case of the killing of Kajunia, described above. Despite the strong evidence that the use of lethal force against Kajunia was wholly unwarranted, no charges have been brought against the police reservist. Apparently, an inquest file was opened by police to record evidence on whether the shooting was justified or not, but no indictment was made against the reservist.[72] Children said that they still see the reservist walking the streets. "The *afande* [the Kiswahili term of respect for police] is still around. He still comes after us and tries to beat us," said street boy Joseph Mwangii.[73] Human Rights Watch sent letters to the attorney general and to the director of CID, inquiring about the status of the inquest, and what measures, if any, are being taken to discipline and prosecute the reservist. As of the date of the printing of this report, no response was received.

In the absence of any visible action on the part of the government to investigate and prosecute the reservist implicated in the shooting of Kajunia, the Kenyan branch of ANPPCAN (African Network for the Prevention and Protection against Child Abuse and Neglect), an NGO, is considering commencing a private criminal action against the police, but has not filed any action to date.[74]

---

[72] "Another street boy slain," *The People* (Nairobi, Kenya), October 3, 1996.

[73] David Orr, "Scandal of the street children that shames Kenya," *The Independent* (United Kingdom), January 27, 1997.

[74] ANPPCAN Kenya is starting up a legal defense unit to provide legal assistance and representation to children, including street children.

IV. ARBITRARY DETENTION

We didn't sleep at all last night. That's why we're sleeping now, during the day. The daytime is our night time. Night is the most dangerous for us. The police come while we're sleeping and catch you off guard, and grab you and hit you. They'll take you to Makadara court [in Eastlands] and then you'll be sent to remand for months. Last night there was a big roundup and we had to move many times to avoid being caught. There was a large group of police in a big lorry, driving around, looking for kids. They're cleaning up the streets now to prepare for the Nairobi International Show [an annual international commerce and trade fair which takes in Nairobi].[75]

Although prohibited under international and Kenyan law, arbitrary detention is a common occurrence throughout Kenya. Street children are particularly vulnerable to this form of detention, as police and local government administrators become increasingly frustrated with their growing presence. Rounding up and locking up street children is viewed as a way to keep the population in check and to clean up the streets, particularly at times of international conferences or during holiday seasons, when national and international attention is focused on a city. Law enforcement and government authorities may also justify roundups as a means to identify children and reunite them with their families or place them in appropriate institutions for their care, although the manner in which the children are treated by police and within the juvenile justice system does not reflect that intention or the realization of that end.

The manner in which street children are detained grossly violates children's fundamental rights. Children often stay in police station lockups for days or even weeks, without being formally charged with an offense, with no assistance to suggest that the child's welfare was a motive for the detention, and without having the legality of their detention reviewed by judicial or other authorities. Children are picked up, held in police lockups where they are often beaten and almost always held with adults, and then released back onto the streets. They are not informed of their rights, not provided with legal counsel, and often beaten by police during questioning and in cells.

---

[75] Human Rights Watch interview with Moses, Nairobi, September 24, 1996.

Arbitrary Detention

International and Kenyan Standards

The Convention on the Rights of the Child, ratified by Kenya in 1990, states that "no child shall be deprived of liberty unlawfully or arbitrarily."[76] The child shall have the right to challenge the legality of the deprivation of his or her liberty before a court or other competent, independent and impartial authority.[77] The U.N. Rules for the Protection of Juveniles Deprived of their Liberty[78] (U.N. Rules for the Protection of Juveniles) mandate that deprivation of liberty should be used only as a measure of last resort, and "for the minimum necessary period and should be limited to exceptional cases" (Rule 2). The U.N. Standard Minimum Rules for the Administration of Juvenile Justice[79] (the Beijing Rules) also require that a judge or other competent official shall, without delay, consider releasing the child instead of recommending further incarceration (Rule 10.2).[80] The child's parent or guardian should be immediately notified of the apprehension of the child, or as soon thereafter as possible (Rule 10.1).

---

[76] Article 37(b) of the Convention on the Rights of the Child provides that: "[n]o child shall be deprived of his or her liberty unlawfully or arbitrarily. The arrest, detention or imprisonment of a child shall be in conformity with the law and shall be used only as a measure of last resort and for the shortest appropriate period of time."

[77] Convention on the Rights of the Child, Article 37(c).

[78] U.N. Rules for the Protection of Juveniles Deprived of their Liberty, G.A. Res. 45/113, annex, 45 U.N. GAOR Supp. (No. 49A) p. 205, U.N. Doc. A/45/49 (1990) ("U.N. Rules for the Protection of Juveniles"). The full text of the U.N. Rules for the Protection of Juveniles are set forth in Appendix C.

[79] U.N. Standard Minimum Rules for the Administration of Juvenile Justice, G.A. Res. 40/33, 40 U.N. GAOR Supp. (No. 53) p. 207, U.N. Doc. A/40/53 (1985) ("Beijing Rules"). The full text of the Beijing Rules are set forth in Appendix B.

[80] The ICCPR, ratified by Kenya in 1976, essentially requires the same for any person deprived of his or her liberty by arrest or detention: Anyone arrested or detained on a criminal charge shall be brought promptly before a judge or other officer authorized by law to exercise judicial power and shall be entitled to trial within a reasonable time or to release. It shall not be the general rule that persons awaiting trial shall be detained in custody, but release may be subject to guarantees to appear for trial, at any other stage of the judicial proceedings, and, should occasion arise, for execution of the judgement (Article 9(3)).

Under Article 29 of the Criminal Procedure Code of Kenya,[81] a police officer has wide powers of arrest without a warrant, including the power to arrest:

> (a) any person whom he suspects upon reasonable grounds of having committed a cognizable offence;
>
> (f) any person whom he finds in a highway, yard, or other place during the night and whom he suspects upon reasonable grounds of having committed or being about to commit a felony; and
>
> (g) any person whom he finds in a street or public place during the hours of darkness and whom he suspects upon reasonable grounds of being there for an illegal or disorderly purpose, or who is unable to give a satisfactory account of himself.

Under the Vagrancy Act, a police officer (including an administration police officer) may also arrest without a warrant "any person who is apparently a vagrant." Under Article 2 of the Vagrancy Act, vagrant is defined, among other things, as:

> (a) a person having neither lawful employment nor lawful means of subsistence such as to provide him regularly with the necessities for his maintenance; or
>
> (b) a person having no fixed abode[82] and not giving a satisfactory account of himself; or
>
> (c) a person wandering abroad, or placing himself in a public place, to beg or gather alms.

The Criminal Procedure Code requires that a person arrested without a warrant be brought "without unnecessary delay" before a magistrate or an officer

---

[81] The Criminal Procedure Code of Kenya, Chapter 75 of the Laws of Kenya.

[82] For the purposes of this paragraph, the Vagrancy Act states that "a person lodging in or about any verandah, pavement, sidewalk, passage, outhouse, shed, warehouse, store, shop or unoccupied building, or in the open air or in or about a cart or vehicle, shall be deemed to be a person having no fixed abode."

in charge of a police station.[83] Officers in charge of police stations must report all arrests without warrants to the nearest magistrate.[84] If the detention is premised on criminal grounds, the constitution requires that the detainee be brought before a court "as soon as is reasonably practicable" and ordinarily within twenty-four hours.[85] Assistant Commissioner of Police Rhoda Kimundi told us that children must ordinarily be brought before a magistrate within twenty-four hours of arrest, unless the arrest takes place on a Friday, in which case children will be held until the following Monday before being brought to court.[76]

If the child "cannot be brought forthwith before a court," the police shall release the child "on a recognizance being entered into by his parent or guardian or other responsible person, with or without sureties" except in cases where the child is charged with a serious crime such as murder or manslaughter; or it is in the interest of the child to remove him or her from association with any undesirable person; or if releasing the child would defeat the ends of justice.[86]

Confinement in Police Lockups

Children are regularly picked up individually by police or are rounded up in groups during street sweeps, for no reason other than the fact that they are homeless or because a theft has occurred in the area. Decisions to round up street children are made by the police, sometimes in conjunction with local government authorities and the Children's Department.[87] "Sometimes the police round up the children on their own initiative, and sometimes I ask them to do it, periodically," said H.O. Miyienda, the provincial children's officer for the Western Province of

---

[83] Criminal Procedure Code, Article 33.

[84] Ibid., Article 37.

[85] Constitution of Kenya, Article 72(3). If the underlying criminal offence is punishable by death, the detainee may be held longer, for up to fourteen days, before being brought before a court.

[86] Children and Young Persons Act, Article 10.

[87] Local government in Kenya is administered through a system which corresponds to the division of the country into eight provinces, further subdivided into districts. Each province is headed by a provincial commissioner, under which are district commissioners, district officers, mayors, city commissioners or councillors, tribal chiefs and sub-chiefs (chiefs are political appointees with no relation to the tribal composition of their area).

Kenya.[88] Other employees of the Children's Department in Nairobi said, "provincial children's officers, in conjunction with provincial commissioners, will decide to round up children and instruct the police. Police sometimes will also liaise with the city commissioner and the city police (city *askaris)* to round up hawkers. Police will also apprehend a child who is found alone."[89] Rhoda Kimundi told us that roundups are conducted for the purpose of helping the children—"to sort out the children, and feed them, and send them back to their families."[90] In practice, most roundups are conducted in a punitive manner, and children may end up being charged with the crime of vagrancy or the status offense of being "in need of protection or discipline" in courts.

Roundups occur most frequently in Nairobi, where the numbers of street children are the highest, and take place usually at night. Group roundups also used to occur with regularity in Kisumu, but had dropped off in 1996 due to NGO pressure on police and local authorities.[91] Regardless, children continue to be picked up frequently at night by police. A fifteen-year-old boy from Ahero town in Kisumu district told us that he had been arrested five times, and that most of the arrests had also occurred at night. His most recent arrest had occurred a few months earlier, in June 1996, when he and other boys were asleep near the bus station in Kisumu. They were arrested by a mixed group of regular police and administrative police, riding in a lorry. Twenty boys were caught and held overnight in the courtyard of the police station, before being taken to court.[92]

The majority of street children whom we interviewed stayed an average of a few days in lockups before being released or taken to court. However, sixteen out of forty-three children who were arrested and held at police stations said they

---

[88] Interview with Provincial Children's Officer for Western Province, H.O. Miyienda, in Kakamega, September 23, 1996. The Children's Department is headed by a director, supported by a staff of provincial children's officers, district children's officers and regular children's officers.

[89] Interview with Bakala Wambani, officer in charge, and John B. Karau, children's officer, Nairobi Juvenile Remand Home, October 4, 1996 ("Interview with staff of Nairobi Juvenile Remand Home").

[90] Interview with the Assistant Commissioner of Police.

[91] Human Rights Watch interview with Alphonse Lumumba, Pandipieri Street Children's Programme, Kisumu, September 21, 1996.

[92] Human Rights Watch interview with Tom, Kisumu, September 22, 1996.

were held in lockups between one week and two months before being released or taken to court: six were held for one week; six were held for two weeks; two were held for three weeks; one was held for one month; and one was held for two months. The excessive duration of periods in lockups is worsened by the fact that conditions in lockups are extremely harmful to children—they are often beaten, almost always held with adults under deplorable physical conditions, and with no form of legal redress. Rarely were children's parents or guardians informed by police of the apprehension of the child.[93] Release on bail to a parent or other responsible person was not extended to any of the street children whom we interviewed.

Physical Abuse by Police

Individual arrests and group roundups are conducted with brute force. Children described being grabbed and kicked, hit and sometimes whipped, caned or clubbed by police. Twenty-five out of forty-five children whom we interviewed and who were arrested, said they had been beaten by police at the time of arrest and/or at the police station. Seven out of the forty-five said they had not been beaten.

The Convention on the Rights of the Child states that children deprived of their liberty "shall be treated with humanity and respect for the inherent dignity of the human person" and that no child "shall be subjected to torture or other cruel, inhuman or degrading treatment or punishment" (Article 37). The Constitution of Kenya, under Article 74(1), prohibits the same.[94] The U.N. Basic Principles on the

---

[93] This may be attributable to the fact that many street children have intermittent or rare contact with family members, who may be difficult to contact or whose whereabouts are unknown.

[94] The Convention Against Torture and Other Cruel, Inhuman, or Degrading Treatment or Punishment (not ratified by Kenya), defines torture as:
> any act by which severe pain or suffering, whether physical or mental, is intentionally inflicted on a person for such purposes as obtaining from him or a third person information or a confession, punishing him for an act he or a third person has committed or is suspected of having committed, or intimidating or coercing him or a third person, . . . when such pain or suffering is inflicted by or at the instigation of or with the consent or acquiescence of a public official or other person acting in an official capacity.

Convention Against Torture and Other Cruel, Inhuman, or Degrading Treatment or Punishment , G.A. Res. 39/46, annex, 39 U.N. GAOR Supp. (No. 51) at 197, U.N. Doc.

Use of Force and Firearms by Law Enforcement Officials contain guidelines on the policing of persons in custody or detention; law enforcement personnel "shall not use force, except when strictly necessary for the maintenance of security and order within the institution, or when personal safety is threatened."[95]

Beatings are commonly used to punish children for being on the streets, or during interrogations to find out information about a child's background, identity or alleged offenses. Sixteen-year-old Morgan, in Kisumu, described his treatment by police when he was arrested for an alleged forgery:

> I was taken to the police station in Maseno market and was put in a cell with about ten men. The first day I was whipped by two policemen in the investigation room. They whipped me while they asked me questions and while two other policemen held me down. I refused to confess to the forgery. On the second day, I was called from my cell into the OCS's [officer in charge of station's] office. The OCS slapped me while he asked me questions. I still denied all the accusations. The OCS then ordered me to kneel on the floor for two hours.[96]

Fifteen-year-old John, from Vihiga district in Western Province, described how he was rounded up by city *askaris* and whipped with a motorcycle cable wire in Kamukunji police station in Nairobi: "Two police men in uniforms questioned me. They asked me questions, like where I was from, where my parents were. Every time I didn't answer a question, they whipped me on my back with a cable brake from a motorcycle."[97]

John also described receiving what he said police called a "welcome" upon first entering the station—a round of kicks, slaps, and hits. Several other children confirmed this practice of "welcoming" children on their first day of lockup. Fourteen-year-old David, from Nyandarua district in Central Province, explained: "usually the first day you're beaten, when they put you in the cell. At that time they'll also hit anyone else who's around. They don't know exactly who

---

A/39/51 (1984).

[95] Basic Principles, Article 15.

[96] Human Rights Watch interview with Morgan, Kisumu, September 20, 1996.

[97] Human Rights Watch interview with John, Kisumu, September 20, 1996.

the new ones are and who the old ones are so anyone might be hit."[98] Seventeen-year-old Minga described his detention one month earlier in Parklands Police Station in Nairobi for us: "I stayed in the cell for three days. The first day, I was hit on the head with a pistol and kicked and punched. Whichever policeman would come into the cell and do the head count would hit me."[99]

It appears that street children may be beaten by police as a way of distributing summary punishment to children and to warn and frighten them into behaving, before releasing them back onto the streets. A social worker from Nairobi commented on the police practice of locking up and beating children:

> The police response is partly administrative convenience: a summary punishment in the form of corporal punishment is meted out and the "delinquent" is released without charges having to be prepared or court proceedings gone through. Often both sides are content with this. Partly it is exasperation at the inability to solve an insoluble problem. . . . The young person may well know that going to court will only set off a procedure which will result in several periods of remand of a much longer duration, no matter what the outcome of the case itself.[100]

Eight out of forty-five children we interviewed, who had been arrested, said that they were released by police at the station without ever being sent on to court. All eight boys who were released said they were beaten, usually whipped or caned, before being released. Two of the eight said they were released on the same day that they were arrested. The other six reported that they spent between five days and two months in lockups before being released by police.

---

[98] Human Rights Watch interview with David, Nairobi, September 17, 1996.

[99] Human Rights Watch interview with Minga, Nairobi, September 17, 1996.

[100] Villoo Nowrojee, "Juvenile Delinquency and an Exploration of the Laws Governing Children in the Criminal Process in Kenya: A Study of a Volunteer Organization—Undugu," paper presented to the Graduate School of Social Work of Bryn Mawr College, May 1990, pp. 46-47.

Physical Conditions in Lockups

The ICCPR requires that "all persons deprived of their liberty shall be treated with humanity and with respect for the inherent dignity of the human person."[101] The Convention on the Rights of the Child requires the same.[102]

The cells in which children are held are often overcrowded, unclean, poorly ventilated, overrun with lice and vermin, and without running water. They are completely bare of any furnishings. All children we interviewed reported that they slept on the floor, usually without even a blanket to cover them. The absence of any bedding material is worsened by the fact that boys and men must usually remove their shirts, along with their shoes and belts, before being put in lockup. Cells were sometimes so crowded that children said they had to sleep sitting up or on their sides, because there was not enough room in the cell to lie down. Children said food was provided one, two, or three times a day, and in small quantities and of poor quality. Usually buckets served as toilets, and if there were toilets attached to the cells, they stank and filled the room with the odor of excrement and urine. Children's descriptions of different police stations are set forth below:

> **Central Police Station in Nairobi**: We were all squashed into the cell, women and girls together. The police hit us with sticks when they put us in the cell. We were squeezed together when we slept on the floor at night. There were no blankets and no mattresses. Nothing. There was a bathroom attached to the cell which we could use whenever we wanted. The toilet smelled. They fed us bad *ugali* [porridge made of maize meal] and *sukuma wiki* [a green leafy vegetable] to eat. I didn't eat it, it looked so bad. Sometimes they gave us water to drink. The police were always yelling at us and checking on us. This one policeman, called Kiragu, beat me. I stayed there for two weeks before I went to court.[103]
>
> **Parklands Police Station in Nairobi**: The first time I was in Parklands station, I stayed there for only one night. I stayed in a cell with drunk ladies, *changga* [home made alcohol] sellers,

---

[101] ICCPR, Article 10(1).

[102] Convention on the Rights of the Child, Article 37(c).

[103] Human Rights Watch interview with Pamela, Nairobi, September 24, 1996.

and two men. We all slept on the floor. They fed us *ugali* and greens. There was a small hall that served as a toilet. That time I wasn't beaten, but some of the others were. The police made one man bend down and put a finger on the floor and run around in circles while another policeman was kicking him. The next time I was arrested I was brought to Parklands again, and stayed for two nights, but this time I stayed in a different cell—it was larger. There were adults and kids there together, but the adults were taken somewhere else at night to sleep. I didn't have any problems with the adults. The only problems I had were with the police. I woke up in the middle of the night to find police beating me with a stick and kicking me. I must have been asleep when they were taking roll call.[104]

We were given toast in the morning and tea without sugar. There was no lunch. In the evening they gave us water and a small amount of *ugali*. We were very hungry. There was no light and no running water, but they gave us drinking water. There were fleas all over the place. We slept on the floor. There were two filthy blankets for all seven of us to share.[105]

Kamukunji Police Station in Nairobi: I was forced to clean the police station when I got there. Then they put me in a small dirty cell with some drunk men and two other boys. The cell mates did not mistreat me. The first day I was beaten by two police with a long wooden stick. They called me names—said I was a thief. They didn't ask me questions, they just beat me. There was no toilet in the cell. I peed on the floor. I was hungry all the time. They fed us a half cup of tea in the morning, and a small portion of *ugali* in the evening. That was it. After a week I was brought to court.[106]

---

[104] Human Rights Watch interview with Zachary, Nairobi, September 24, 1996.

[105] Human Rights Watch interview with Peter, Nairobi, September 17, 1996.

[106] Human Rights Watch interview with Andrew, Nairobi, September 17, 1996.

I was put in a separate room for children in Kamukunji. There were no windows and the room was dark and crowded. There was no light aside from what light came through the sheeting on the ceiling. There was a bucket for a toilet. Sometimes they let the kids out to get water. I was hungry. They fed us once a day, *ugali* and *sukuma wiki* at night. They also gave us a cup of tea in the morning. Two police men in uniforms questioned me. They asked me questions, like where I was from, where my parents were. Every time I didn't answer a question, they whipped me on my back with a cable brake from a motorcycle. After two months there, they let me go. I never went to court.[107]

Central Police Station in Mombasa: The cell was small and damp. There were between twelve and twenty people in the cell when I was there. I was the only kid. There were bedbugs and lice. There was only one window and it was very high up. There was nothing in the cell. We slept on the floor. The lights were on twenty-four hours a day. There was a bucket for a toilet. They gave us tea and a slice of bread in the morning, *ugali* and greens for lunch, and the same thing again for dinner with a little water to drink.[108]

Police Station in Likoni *(near Mombasa)*: There was only one cell and there were around sixty people in it. We were all mixed together, adults and kids, but the women stayed separately in the corridor. It was so crowded I had to sleep sitting up, with my knees pulled up to my chest. There was a bucket for a toilet, and no running water in the cell. There were no windows and the place smelled. There was a small hole in the door which was the only place where light came in. In the morning they fed us half a cup of tea and two slices of bread. For lunch they gave us a little *ugali* and cabbage, and the same thing for dinner.[109]

---

[107] Human Rights Watch interview with John, Kisumu, September 20, 1996.

[108] Human Rights Watch interview with Tom, Mombasa, September 28, 1996.

[109] Human Rights Watch interview with Jack, Mombasa, September 28, 1996.

Police Station in Kisumu: The cell was dirty, with a bucket for a toilet . . . . The cell had two small windows with bars and mosquito netting. There were no lights in the room. There were no blankets, nothing at all to sleep on. They fed us twice a day. In the morning they gave us tea and bread, and for supper we got *ugali* and *sukuma wiki*. There was water available in a separate room, which we could get to if we wanted.[110]

The cell was small and crowded and adults and kids were mixed together. There were no lights, and no windows, only small vents with wire mesh over them. There was one small window in the door of the cell that faced onto the corridor. There was a bucket for a toilet. The food wasn't enough. They gave us one piece of toast and tea in the morning, and a small portion of *ugali* and *sukuma wiki* for lunch. There was no dinner. At midnight they'd take roll call, and if you didn't answer you'd be caned. We slept on the floor sitting up because there wasn't room to lie down. There were lice on the floor, you could see them.[111]

Children Held with Adults
An overwhelming majority of the children we interviewed who had been arrested were locked in cells with adults despite the clear standards in international law that children should never be held with adults. Article 10(1)(b) of the ICCPR and Rules 13.4 and 26.3 of the Beijing Rules require that children suspected of offenses be separated from adults if detained. The Kenyan Children and Young Persons act requires that children under the age of sixteen be detained separately from adults in police stations and while being conveyed between police station and court, and while waiting to attend or leave any court.[112] In this regard, Kenyan law

---

[110] Human Rights Watch interview with Augustine, Kisumu, September 21, 1996.

[111] Human Rights Watch interview with Andrew, Kisumu, September 22, 1996.

[112] An exception to this rule exists for children under the age of sixteen who are jointly charged with adults for the same offense. They may be detained and tried with adults. Children and Young Persons Act, Article 6.
The Children and Young Persons Act divides children into three categories by age: "child" refers to children thirteen years old and younger; "juvenile" refers to fourteen and

is inconsistent with international standards, including the Convention on the Rights of the Child, which require that persons under the age of eighteen not be detained with adult offenders.[113]

When questioned about the regular practice of detaining children with adults, Assistant Commissioner of Police Rhoda Kimundi responded, "it could be that the cells were too full. Children should not be mixed with adults unless it is something that cannot be avoided."[114] Commingling was found to be the norm, and separation the exception. Three out of forty-three children we interviewed, who were arrested and held at the police station, told us they were held in a separate room or area for children. Thirty told us they were mixed with adults. Almost all were separated by sex.

None of the children we interviewed complained about mistreatment by adult cell mates. However, children commonly complained that police singled them out from adults to perform chores around the station, such as cleaning out waste buckets, and cleaning offices in the station. Fourteen-year-old Augustine, from Kisumu district, told us how he had been caught in a roundup at night along with four other boys, and taken to the police station in Kisumu:

> The police caned us and took us to the station. I stayed there for one week. There were men and kids mixed together. Women were in a separate room. The cell was dirty, with a bucket for a toilet. Us kids were made to clean out the bucket every morning, and to clean the shit and urine off the floor.[115]

Another fourteen-year-old boy told us that in the Central Police Station in Mombasa he was held in a cell with between twelve and twenty adults for six nights. He complained, "the police bullied me because I was the only young boy

---

fifteen year-olds; and "young person" refers to sixteen and seventeen-year-olds (Article 2). Young persons are accorded a lower standard of protection than juveniles or children under Kenyan law.

[113] Convention on the Rights of the Child, Article 37(c).

[114] Interview with the Assistant Commissioner of Police.

[115] Human Rights Watch interview with Augustine, Kisumu, September 21, 1996.

there. They made me mop the offices, and clean up the other cells. The others didn't have to do this."[116]

After spending several nights or weeks under these conditions, children are released or taken to court.

---

[116] Human Rights Watch interview with Tom, Mombasa, September 28, 1996.

V. PROCEDURES FOR CONFINING STREET CHILDREN IN INSTITUTIONS

I was charged along with four other girls who I didn't know. We hadn't been arrested together but we were all on the same charge sheet. They read us the charges, 'loitering with intent to solicit.' We didn't have a lawyer. The magistrate told us it would be better for us if we pleaded guilty, so we pled guilty. We were sentenced to two weeks in Langata prison, or to pay a fine of 1000 shillings. The whole thing lasted about five minutes.[117]

Street children are frequently arrested by police and brought before courts where they are charged with criminal offenses or classified as being "in need of "protection or discipline." Without representation by legal counsel, and without the presence of a parent or legal guardian, these children are subjected to brief hearings on their cases whereby they may be deprived of their liberty and committed for years to juvenile correctional institutions know as approved schools or borstal institutions. Under Kenyan law, children fourteen years old and above also may be committed to regular prisons, although this practice is reportedly rare. Before they are committed to these institutions, children frequently spend excessive periods in temporary detention centers, called juvenile remand homes or remand prisons, pending adjudication of their cases. This section will focus on the procedures by which children are confined to these institutions.

Juvenile Court

The primary law in Kenya concerning children in conflict with the law is the Children and Young Persons Act. The court system in Kenya is three-tiered and consists of a court of appeals, a high court, and lower courts known as magistrate's courts. The Children and Young Persons Act establishes juvenile courts, at the level of magistrates' courts, for the purpose of hearing all charges against persons under eighteen years of age, except in cases where children are

---

[117] Human Rights Watch interview with Elizabeth, Nairobi, October 2, 1996. Given Elizabeth's age, fifteen at the time of arrest, she should have been brought to the Juvenile Law Court and not City Court.

charged jointly with adults.[118] If a child is brought before a regular court and it becomes apparent that the person is under eighteen years of age, the court must remit the case to juvenile court.[119] Juvenile courts must sit in a different building or on different days or at different times from regular courts for adults, and are closed to the general public.[120] Only one separate juvenile court exists in Kenya, the Juvenile Law Court in Nairobi, presided over by Magistrate Dixon Konya. Other *ad hoc* juvenile courts are convened in regular courthouses throughout Kenya; the courtrooms are cleared of adults before children's cases are heard, or the cases are heard *in camera*.[121]

Despite the requirement that children's cases be heard in juvenile courts, sixteen out of forty children that we interviewed who were brought to court, said their cases were heard in regular courts mixed with adult cases. None of the children we interviewed were charged jointly with adults.[122] Children arrested in or around Nairobi described being taken to City Court, Makadara Court, and High Court (instead of the Juvenile Law Court) where they were mixed with adults. Outside of Nairobi, where *ad hoc* juvenile courts are convened, children reported that their cases were heard in open court rooms mixed with adults.

---

[118] Children and Young Persons Act, Article 3(1). Cases where children are charged jointly with adults will be heard in regular courts for adults.

[119] Ibid., Article 13(1).

[120] Ibid., Article 4. It should be noted that under Article 14 of the Penal Code, children under the age of eight are not criminally responsible for any act or omission. A person under the age of twelve is not criminally responsible for an act or omission, unless it is proved that the child had the capacity to know that he ought not to do the act or make the omission.

[121] Human Rights Watch interview with Erich Oluoch Ogwang, former magistrate of Juvenile Law Court in Nairobi, September 26, 1996 ("Interview with former magistrate of the Juvenile Law Court"); J.M. Mbiti, "The Role and Procedure in Juvenile Court," Report of the Workshop on Criminal Justice and Children, held at Kenya Institute of Administration, Nairobi, April 7-11, 1986 ("The Role and Procedure in Juvenile Court"), p. 46.

[122] Recall that the Children and Young Persons Act authorizes the trial of children in regular courts if they are charged jointly with adults (Article 3(1)).

A representative of an NGO that works with street children in Nairobi explained how children might be processed as adults and pointed to the critical role that police play in determining which court a child is sent to:

> Police have huge discretion in deciding what court you go to. They write the charge sheet and they take you to court. If they think you're older or if the offense is a more serious one, they'll take you to regular court. It's all based on looks. Kids can't explain themselves to the police. There's no time, and they're scared.[123]

Njuguna Mutahi, of the Kenya Human Rights Commission, similarly commented:

> Police decide your age, basically on your looks, and they can make mistakes. There are other problems too—like in rural areas pastoralist children are born at home and have no official registration and may not know their exact age. The police don't care. The magistrates don't care. It especially effects street children who don't have concerned parties to complain on their behalf and point out that they're only children.[124]

Even in the Juvenile Law Court, the one juvenile court in Kenya that is housed in its own building, adult cases are also heard. Reportedly this practice developed during the tenure of the last magistrate, who began asking for adult cases to be brought to court.[125] According to probation officers at the court, "she decided hearing only juvenile cases was boring."[126] Whatever the reasons were, the practice has continued to the present.

---

[123] Human Rights Watch interview with NGO representative, Nairobi, September 19, 1996, anonymity requested.

[124] Interview with Kenya Human Rights Commission.

[125] Interview with former magistrate of the Juvenile Law Court.

[126] Interview with probation officers, the Juvenile Law Court, Nairobi, September 16, 1996, anonymity requested ("Interview with probation officers of the Juvenile Law Court").

In the Juvenile Law Court, children's cases are heard at separate times from adult cases. Children are crowded into one of the court's two holding cells, located in an enclosed courtyard behind the main court building. At the time of our visit, on September 17, 1996, the holding cell in which children were kept was completely dark, without any windows or light. There were small air vents at the top where the ceiling met the wall. The only light which came into the cell was through a tiny window in the heavy door. There were approximately forty children in a room of about twenty-five-by-fifteen-feet in size.

Despite Kenyan legal requirements that children's cases be heard in juvenile courts, police and magistrates commonly overlook or neglect to enforce them. There is a clear need for the establishment of more separate juvenile courts throughout Kenya, presided over by magistrates who are specially trained to deal with children's cases. Many NGOs voiced concern over the complete absence of training for magistrates on how to deal with the special needs of children. In areas where it is impractical to establish separate juvenile courts, at least magistrates should ensure that children who come before them are not treated and tried as adults. Police and magistrates should make greater efforts to ascertain the true age of young people in their work, and ensure that children are identified and dealt with as children, in juvenile courts according to law.

Jurisdiction of Juvenile Courts

Jurisdiction of the juvenile courts is broad and extends to "any offence other than manslaughter or an offence punishable by death."[127] In addition to criminal offenses, jurisdiction of the juvenile court extends to non-criminal cases of children under the age of sixteen who are "in need of protection or discipline."[128]

"Protection or discipline" cases refer to the cases of children under the age of sixteen who are uncontrollable, parentless, deserted, destitute, vagrants, beggars or who fall into "bad associations."[129] "Protection or discipline" cases are

---

[127] Children and Young Persons Act, Article 12(1).

[128] Ibid., Article 20. Related to the "protection or discipline" of children, the juvenile court also has jurisdiction over related charges of neglect against parents or guardians. Ibid, Article 23.

[129] Under Article 21 of the Children and Young Persons Act, a child "in need of protection or discipline" is defined as anyone fifteen years old and below:
a) who has no parent or guardian, or has been deserted by his parent or

essentially status offenses,[130] and are subdivided into cases of children "in need of protection and care" (P&C cases) and children "in need of protection and discipline" (P&D cases).[131] Street children's cases are frequently processed as P&D cases.

Confusing overlaps exist between criminal offenses and "protection or discipline" matters. For example, a child vagrant may be a criminal offender under the Vagrancy Act, and may also be a child "in need of protection or discipline" under the Children and Young Persons Act. Similarly, under certain circumstances a child found begging may be an "idle and disorderly person" or a "rogue and

> guardian, or is destitute or a vagrant; or
> b) who cannot be controlled by his parent or guardian; or
> c) whose parent or guardian does not, or is unable or unfit to, exercise proper care and guardianship; or
> d) who is falling into bad associations or is exposed to moral or physical danger; or
> e) who is being kept in any premises which, in the opinion of a medical officer, are overcrowded, insanitary or dangerous; or
> f) who is prevented from receiving compulsory education, or is an habitual truant; or
> g) who frequents any public bar or gambling house, or who is found buying or receiving or in possession of any drug which is deemed to be dangerous or habit forming; or
> h) who is found begging or receiving alms or inducing the giving of alms, whether or not there is any pretense of singing, playing or performing.

[130] Status offenses are offenses which would not be punishable if committed by an adult, such as truancy, running away from home, or being beyond parental control.

[131] Human Rights Watch interview with Karen Ogoti, children's officer assigned to the Juvenile Law Court, Nairobi, September 30, 1996; Human Rights Watch interview with Dixon Konya, magistrate in charge of the Juvenile Law Court, Nairobi, September 30 and October 2, 1996 ("Interview with current magistrate of the Juvenile Law Court.") The difference between children "in need of protection and care" and children "in need of protection and discipline" was explained as follows: the former are usually children who have been abandoned, abused or neglected by their families, whereas the latter are "delinquents." A P&D case is very similar to a criminal case, explained Magistrate Dixon Konya.

vagabond" under the Penal Code,[132] and may also be a child "in need of protection or discipline" under the Children and Young Persons Act. Children from both categories are mixed together in police lockups, in court, in remand, and in approved schools (to which children from both categories may be finally committed). Thus, the distinction between children charged with criminal offenses and children "in need of protection or discipline" is obscured and the categorization is in many ways arbitrary; the legal system essentially treats them the same.

Indeed, street children themselves appear to be unaware of the distinction between criminal and non-criminal status offenses for which they are brought to court, and generally view court proceedings to which they are subjected as criminal. It is no wonder, considering that street children are apprehended and beaten by police, held in lockups usually with adult criminal offenders, and processed often in regular courts. They are further detained in remand homes or in adult remand prisons, and finally may be confined for years in correctional institutions where criminal offenders are mixed with those "in need of protection or discipline." The language the children used to describe their experiences in court reflects their view of the proceedings as criminal. Although the words "conviction" and "sentence" are not to be used to refer to decisions in juvenile court,[133] children told us that they were "guilty" or "not guilty," even when the facts surrounding their apprehension indicated that they were children "in need of protection or discipline."

Referral of Cases to Juvenile Court

Any authorized officer who has reasonable grounds to believe that a child is "in need of protection or discipline" can apprehend a child without a warrant and bring him or her before a court.[134] Authorized officers include: a police officer (including administrative police), a children's officer, an approved officer, a chief or a sub-chief. Police apprehend children on the street for vagrancy or upon suspicion of having committed minor criminal offenses and bring them to court. The Children's Department (under the Ministry of Home Affairs) is charged under the Children and Young Persons Act with the protection and care of children and employs approximately seventy children's officers who investigate cases of

---

[132] Penal Code, Articles 182-83.

[133] Children and Young Persons Act, Article 15.

[134] Report of the 1989 National Conference, p.48.

children at risk or who are "in need of protection or discipline."[135] Among their many duties, children's officers can bring cases of children "in need of protection or discipline" to court, and can apply for an order committing a child to an institution for the child's rehabilitation and welfare. Approved officers are individuals who are appointed by voluntary organizations that are "approved" by the minister of home affairs to work on issues related to the protection and care of children. Chiefs and sub-chiefs are the lowest level of local government administrators, who work under city commissions. They also may bring children's cases to juvenile court. Parents and private citizens can also bring children directly to police or to children's officers for court referral. Parents occasionally do this out of desire to have their child receive a free education in an approved school,[136] reflecting more on the limited opportunities for children on the outside, than on the quality or conditions in approved schools.

Through occasional meetings of local bodies known as district children's advisory committees, police, children's officers, NGOs and local government authorities sometimes work together on issues of common concern, in tracing children's families and alerting each other to the presence of children "in need of protection or discipline."[137] However, by far the most common route of referral to court is through the police.

Rights of the Accused

International and Kenyan Standards

The Convention on the Rights of the Child, ratified by Kenya in 1990, directly addresses the rights of children accused of having infringed penal laws in Article 40 and guarantees, at a minimum, the right to "legal or other appropriate

---

[135] Human Rights Watch interview with Director of Children's Services S. Ole Kwallah, Children's Department, Nairobi, October 4, 1996 ("Interview with Director of Children's Department").

[136] Human Rights Watch interview with Alphonse Lumumba, Pandipieri Street Children's Programme, Kisumu, September 21, 1996. See Section II of this report for a discussion on the costs of public education.

[137] Ibid. The work of district children's advisory committees has met with mixed reviews by NGOs. While their efforts are lauded by some, some have criticized the committees for not meeting frequently enough and even for attempting to control the work of NGOs working with street children.

assistance in the preparation and presentation of his or her defense," including "free assistance of an interpreter if the child cannot understand or speak the language used," not to be compelled to give testimony or confess guilt, and to have the matter determined "without delay" by an independent judicial body, or other independent and impartial authority, in a fair hearing according to law, in the presence of a parent or guardian and "legal or other appropriate assistance." Where a decision is made that a child has infringed penal laws, the child has the right to have that decision and any measures imposed in consequence reviewed by a higher competent, independent and impartial authority.

The Beijing Rules also guarantee basic procedural safeguards to children accused of criminal offenses, "such as the presumption of innocence, the right to be notified of the charges, the right to remain silent, the right to counsel, the right to the presence of a parent or guardian, the right to confront and cross-examine witnesses and the right to appeal to a higher authority."[138] The Beijing Rules also extend these protections to children accused of status offenses, "who may be proceeded against for any specific behaviour that would not be punishable if committed by an adult," such as family disobedience.[139] The very recognition of status offenses as punishable conduct is strongly discouraged by the U.N. Guidelines for the Prevention of Juvenile Delinquency (the Riyadh Guidelines), which recommends that governments should enact legislation prohibiting the very recognition of status offenses.[140]

The Criminal Procedure Code and Constitution of Kenya provide certain protections to any person accused of a criminal offense, including the rights: to defend him or herself in court through a legal representative of his or her choice;[141]

---

[138] Beijing Rules, Rule 7.1.

[139] Ibid., Rule 3.1 and commentary to Rule 3.

[140] Article 56 of the Riyadh Guidelines provides that "legislation should be enacted to ensure that any conduct not considered an offense or not penalized if committed by an adult is not considered an offense and not penalized if committed by a young person." U.N. Guidelines for the Prevention of Juvenile Delinquency, G.A. Res. 45/112, annex, 45, U.N. GAOR Supp. (No. 49A) at 201, U.N. Doc. A/45/49 (1990) ("Riyadh Guidelines").

[141] Constitution of Kenya, Article 77(2)(d); Criminal Procedure Code, Article 193. However, the accused is not entitled to legal representation at public expense except in capital cases. Constitution, Article 77(14).

to examine in person or by legal counsel the witnesses against him or her;[142] to be tried by an impartial court;[143] and to an appeal.[144] "The procedure of hearing juvenile cases [in juvenile courts] is the same as other courts in that the criminal procedure and law of evidence must be followed."[145] As for children, the attendance of the child's parent or guardian may be required during all proceedings, if the parent can be found and resides at a reasonable distance.[146]

Kenyan law, however, does not extend these basic protections to status offenders; this is especially problematic for street children who are often brought before courts without being charged with criminal offenses, who are "children in need of protection or discipline." As such, they are without many of the rights supposedly enjoyed by children charged with criminal offenses, in contravention of international law. In practice, however, both categories of children rarely are able to exercise these rights.

Kenyan Practice

We observed proceedings in the Juvenile Law Court in Nairobi on two separate occasions. Juvenile court proceedings are closed to the public—the only people allowed in the court room are the parties to the case, their attorneys and witnesses, parents or guardians, the magistrate, probation officers and children's officers, the police prosecutor, court clerks, and any other person that the court may specially authorize to be present. The magistrate in charge of the court, Dixon Konya, allowed Human Rights Watch to attend court sessions on two mornings,

---

[142] Ibid., Article 77(2)(e).

[143] Ibid., Article 77(1).

[144] *See* Criminal Procedure Code, Articles 347-379; Children and Young Persons Act, Article 75. Under the Children and Young Persons Act, a child or his or her parents can appeal a juvenile court's decision to confine the child in an approved school. In this respect, a child who is "in need of protection or discipline," who is ordered to be committed to an approved school, has a right of appeal on that decision. Children "in need of protection or discipline" have no right of appeal from any other juvenile court decisions, as they do not enjoy the same protections as children accused of criminal offenses.

[145] The Role and Procedure in Juvenile Court, p. 46.

[146] Children and Young Persons Act, Article 9.

when "mentions" were being heard.[147] Mentions are essentially arraignments or preliminary hearings, and last no longer than a few minutes per case. However, many children's cases never move beyond the mention phase, as will be discussed below.

The Beijing Rules state that proceedings "shall be conducted in an atmosphere of understanding, which shall allow the juvenile to participate therein and to express herself or himself freely."[148] However, we found the atmosphere of the court room to be intimidating and frightening for children, as well as rushed. Thirteen-year-old Peter, from Nairobi, said of his experiences in the Juvenile Law Court "it's like the judge has already made up his mind that you're guilty, from the moment he asks you the first question."[149] *Ad hoc* juvenile court proceedings are also reported to be conducted in an intimidating manner:

> [M]ost court officers do not conduct themselves as they should in Juvenile Court. For a start, there is only one Juvenile Court in the whole country -- in Nairobi. In all other stations, the magistrates have to convene these courts as special sessions of the ordinary courts. This they normally do without regard to the provisions of the law regarding the conduct of a children's court. As a result, children in these courts are subjected to great fear, as prosecutors, advocates, and other court officers addressing them in an intimidating manner in order to get them to make admissions.[150]

On each morning in the Juvenile Law Court, we observed that the children were brought in from the holding cell of the court in a large group and crowded onto benches in the court room. There was barely enough room on the benches to accommodate the forty-five and forty-nine children on each day. Many had been brought directly from the police station and others had been brought from remand. Almost all appeared to be street children. They ranged in age from the very young, about six years old, to adolescents. They all looked dirty, dressed in ragged and

---

[147] We were not able to observe trials of criminal cases.

[148] Beijing Rules, Rule 14.2

[149] Human Rights Watch interview with Peter, Nairobi, September 17, 1996.

[150] ANPPCAN, *Hearing on Street Children in Kenya*, p. 33.

soiled clothes, and many were barefoot. The proceedings took place at a rapid pace with no more than a few minutes spent on each case.

The new cases of children brought directly from the police station were called first. The most frequent charge against children on both days was vagrancy. Cases were called one at a time. Each child would rise from the bench and step forward to be questioned by the magistrate who was seated behind a desk on a raised platform at the head of the court room. The magistrate would ask the children where they were from, where they lived, where their parents were, and if the children had any money. Often visibly frightened, the children sometimes did not respond to questions, or responded inaudibly, to which the magistrate would command them to speak louder.[151] At times the magistrate lost his temper, and sharply scolded children or warned them that if they were found on the streets again they would be jailed.

Referral of cases to children's officers or probation officers

If the case was a "protection or discipline" matter, the magistrate would refer the case to a children's officer for preparation of an "investigation report" (the equivalent of a social inquiry report), and tell the child to sit down. If the "protection or discipline" case was old, and had already been assigned to a children's officer, the officer would rise and present the recommendations of the investigation report (on what correctional measure to order). Often the investigation report was not ready and the officer would request more time for its preparation.

If the charge was a criminal offense, the magistrate would ask for the plea. In City Court[152] in Nairobi, where sixteen-year-old Elizabeth was taken a year earlier, she described being advised by the magistrate to plead guilty: "It would be better" for her, she was told by the magistrate.[153]

---

[151] The accounts that the children gave of their own situations varied. Some said they had come to the city to look for family members, that they were lost, or that they were doing errands when they were picked up by police. Others said they lived on the streets.

[152] The City Court in Nairobi is located in city hall, and hears cases involving violations of city council bylaws, which include "loitering with intent to solicit." The City Court is presided over by the same magistrates as in regular courts.

[153] Human Rights Watch interview with Elizabeth, Nairobi, October 2, 1996. Given Elizabeth's age, she should have been brought to the Juvenile Law Court and not the City Court.

Once an admission of guilt was entered, the magistrate would assign a probation officer to the case for the preparation of a "pre-sentencing report." If the case was old, and a probation officer had already been assigned to the case, the officer would rise and present the recommendation on sentencing to the magistrate. If the child pled "not guilty," a court date would be set for the child to reappear for another mention or for trial.

Translation and explanation of proceedings

The proceedings were conducted in Kiswahili and English. Occasionally a child would be called who spoke neither, and one of the court officers would interpret portions of the proceedings for the child. However, occasionally interpreters are not available, as was the case for fourteen-year-old Gordon. He told us how two years earlier he had been rounded up off the streets and brought to the Juvenile Law Court:

> The judge spoke to me in Kiswahili but I didn't understand. I only speak Luo. People in the court room started laughing at me. The judge motioned for me to sit down. At the end, I was brought to his chambers, and he spoke to me again in Kiswahili. Then he caned me. From there I was sent to Kabete remand [Nairobi Juvenile Remand].[154]

On the days we observed proceedings in the Juvenile Law Court, the magistrate made efforts to explain to children what was happening to them (where they were being sent, what correctional measures he was ordering, or when they would have to reappear in court). However, several children we interviewed told us that in other courts they were not informed of the status of their cases, were confused about the nature and purpose of the proceedings, and were unaware of the disposition of their cases. For example, fifteen-year-old Tom told us of his first experience in the High Court in Kisumu in June 1996, after he was rounded up while sleeping near the bus station:

> No one talked to me or explained anything that was happening. The magistrate asked me where I was from, and why I had left home. He didn't tell me what he had decided for me. I figured he had decided to send me to remand, where most kids get sent,

---

[154] Human Rights Watch interview with Simon, Mombasa, September 28, 1996.

and I was right. I was taken to juvenile remand home where I stayed for three days, and was then just released."[155]

Similarly, another street boy in Kisumu expressed his confusion over court proceedings, after he was charged with being a "rogue and vagabond":

From the Central Police Station in Kisumu I was brought to court and sent to Kodiaga remand prison. . . . I went back to court three times, every two weeks. The first time I went, the judge wasn't there. I was brought into a room and was questioned by some people. I don't know who they were. After another two weeks, it was the same procedure again. Then the third time I went back I saw the judge. He turned me over to the police and they brought me to the Central Police Station. I didn't know what was happening. The judge didn't tell me anything. Then from the police station, the police took me to Kiambu and left me with my parents.[156]

Presence of parent or guardian

Parents or guardians were rarely present at the proceedings that we observed. Only five out of forty children we interviewed, who had appeared in court, said that a parent or guardian had been present for a part of the court proceedings. In the Juvenile Law Court, we observed that parents must wait outside the courtroom in the hallway and are called in when their child's case is called. A representative of a street children's NGO in Nairobi told us that sometimes cases were called so quickly that it was possible for a parent to miss the case entirely.[157] Once in the courtroom, the parents appeared to be as intimidated as the children before the magistrate. In non-criminal cases, the child was released to the parent then and there if the parent was willing to accept the child. In one case that we observed, however, the parent told the magistrate that she did not want the boy released to her because she could not control him. The boy broke down in

---

[155] Human Rights Watch interview with Tom, Kisumu, September 22, 1996.

[156] Human Rights Watch interview with Simon, Mombasa, September 28, 1996.

[157] Human Rights Watch interview with NGO representative, Nairobi, September 19, 1996, anonymity requested.

tears as the magistrate announced that the boy was a "delinquent" and would be sent to an approved school.

Legal or other assistance

None of the children on either days were represented by attorneys, and none of the forty children we interviewed, who had appeared in court, had legal counsel at any time. Legal representation is so rare that two probation officers attached to the Juvenile Law Court told us the last case they remembered where a child had legal counsel was sometime the year before, in 1995.[158] Eric Oluoch Ogwang, a former magistrate of the Juvenile Law Court, explained that very few parents can even afford to come to court in Nairobi, let alone afford to hire an attorney for their children.[159] He said that during his tenure he often found himself in the awkward position of trying to play both the role of children's advocate and judge, especially for children charged with criminal offenses whose cases are prosecuted in court by police prosecutors.[160]

Considering that street children are rarely if ever represented by attorneys, whether charged with criminal or non-criminal offenses, it is no surprise that they do not exercise the right to appeal. Probation officers attached to the Juvenile Law Court told us, "kids don't think of appealing, they think of escaping. Even if they're told that they have fourteen days to appeal, they don't, they just think of escaping. They don't even understand what appealing means."

A number of NGOs said they would like to apply to have their own social workers recognized by the Children's Department as approved officers, which would enable them to speak on behalf of children in juvenile court. As mentioned earlier, approved officers are individuals who must be "approved" by the minister of home affairs ("gazetted" by the Children's Department) to work on issues related to the protection and care of children. They are authorized to bring children's cases to court and to appear in court on behalf of children "in need of protection or discipline." "We need our own approved officers to represent our

---

[158] Interview with probation officers of the Juvenile Law Court.

[159] Interview with former magistrate of the Juvenile Law Court.

[160] As mentioned earlier in this report (in Section III), police prosecutors are police who are specially trained to prosecute lower level criminal cases in courts. When they appear in juvenile court they dress in civilian clothing, "to not frighten the children," Magistrate Dixon Konya told us. Very serious criminal cases are prosecuted by state counsel under the Attorney General's Office.

children when they appear in juvenile court," said Josephine Mulli, the head of community organization at the Undugu Society of Kenya.[161] A number of NGOs complained that the process of being "gazetted" was overly difficult and recommended that the procedure be simplified in the interest of enabling social workers who work with street children to provide assistance to children in court proceedings. Easing restrictions for gazetting approved officers would enable NGOs working with street children to assist children in court, and would also allow NGOs greater access to children in institutions, which they are currently denied.

Committal to Remand Detention

International law requires that "[d]etention before trial shall be avoided to the extent possible and limited to exceptional circumstances . . . . When preventive detention is nevertheless used, juvenile courts and investigative bodies shall give the highest priority to the most expeditious processing of such cases to ensure the shortest possible duration of detention."[162] Whenever possible, detention pending trial should be replaced by alternative measures.

Under Kenyan law, pending adjudication of a case, courts may order that children be detained in either a juvenile remand home or a remand prison, depending on the age and behavior of the child. Children under the age of fourteen are to be detained in juvenile remand homes, which are under the administration of the Children's Department.[163] Fourteen- and fifteen-year-olds may be detained in either juvenile remand homes or in remand prisons for adults if the court finds that the child "is of so unruly a character that he cannot safely be remanded in custody to a juvenile remand home."[164] Sixteen- and seventeen-year-old children are to be remanded to adult remand prisons, which are under the administration of the Prisons Department.

---

[161] Interview with Undugu Society of Kenya.

[162] U.N. Rules for the Protection of Juveniles, Rule 17; *see also* Beijing Rules, Rule 13; Convention on the Rights of the Child, Article 37(b).

[163] In the event that there is no juvenile remand home within a reasonable distance of the court, the court can make alternative custodial orders as it deems fit. *See* Children and Young Persons Act, Article 11.

[164] Ibid.

Kenyan courts almost always order that street children be remanded pending final adjudication of a case. Out of forty street children we interviewed who had been brought before courts, thirty-five were detained in remand pending adjudication of their cases or execution of their sentences. The five who were not remanded were discharged. Among the children who were remanded, two were remanded to police stations where they stayed for one week before being finally committed to an approved school or borstal institution. Nine were remanded to adult remand prisons, where several were held with adults; they were between twelve and seventeen years old at the time.[165] The rest were remanded to juvenile remand homes.

There are no limits under Kenyan law on the period of remand, so long as the child reappears in court every two weeks for a mention.[166] Periods of remand usually vary from a few days to several weeks or months, and occasionally years. Six out of the thirty-five children we interviewed who were remanded spent over six months in remand before they were finally committed to permanent correctional facilities or received a final disposition on their case. Two had been in remand for over a year and were still in remand at the time of our interviews. On our visit to Nairobi Juvenile Remand Home (known as Kabete) staff told us that "some kids have been here for three years, about ten kids have been here since 1994."[167]

One reason for the detention of children in remand homes for excessive periods of time is that children's officers do not complete their investigation reports in a timely manner. An officer preparing a report must interview the child and, where possible, the child's family members. Sometimes a trip to the child's home village is required. Further children's officers are generally overworked; preparing investigation reports for children "in need of protection or discipline" is only one

---

[165] It should be noted that two boys told us that police took them directly to adult remand prisons upon arrest (Industrial Area Remand and Shimolatewa Remand) instead of to the police station. Although legally a court order is needed to place a child in a remand home or remand prison, occasionally police will send children directly from the street to remand for holding. According to the former magistrate of the Juvenile Law Court, Eric Ogwang, this occurs when police stations are overcrowded and cannot accommodate children.

[166] Interview with current magistrate of the Juvenile Law Court; Interview with former magistrate of the Juvenile Law Court.

[167] Human Rights Watch interview with Bakala Wambani, officer in charge, and Children's Officer John B. Karau, staff of Nairobi Juvenile Remand Home, Nairobi, October 4, 1996 ("Interview with staff of Nairobi Juvenile Remand Home").

of many duties of children's officers. On one of the days that we attended court, a children's officer told us that she and another officer had been assigned twenty P&C cases that day alone.[168] Sometimes probation officers are called upon by courts to prepare reports for children "in need of protection or discipline," to relieve some of the burden which would otherwise fall on children's officers.[169] Still, we found that many children fall through the cracks, and spend months in remand before their investigation reports are ready.

Another reason for delays, in the cases of children who have pled "not guilty" to criminal offenses, may be that the prosecution has not been able to prepare its case against the child. "The law does not stipulate the period within which the trial of a charged suspect must begin. The Government has acknowledged cases in which persons have been held in pretrial detention for several years, usually because of backlogs."[170] Witnesses or other concerned parties may not be available, or might not show up for the hearing date. One boy we interviewed in Likoni Juvenile Remand told us "I've been here for three years. I go to court every two weeks. I was accused of stealing a bed cover, but there's no evidence against me, because the police didn't bring the bed cover in."[171]

Fully aware of the often lengthy periods of remand which follow a plea of "not guilty," many children plead guilty to criminal charges because they know the remand period is likely to be shorter. After a guilty plea is entered, a probation officer is assigned to the case and usually issues a pre-sentencing report within a period of two to four weeks. Upon the admission of guilt, magistrates sometimes decide sentences on the spot, if the offense is a minor one. Probation officers at the Juvenile Law Court explained:

---

[168] Interview with Children's Officer Karen Ogoti, the Juvenile Law Court, Nairobi, September 30, 1996.

[169] Interview with probation officers of the Juvenile Law Court; Human Rights Watch interview with Director of Probation and After Care Services Department Joseph K. Gitau, Nairobi, September 18, 1996.

[170] U.S. Department of State, Kenya Country Report on Human Rights Practices for 1996, Section 1(d).

[171] Human Rights Watch interview with Mugambi, Likoni Juvenile Remand Home, September 27, 1996.

Some children just plead guilty because they think things will happen faster. They don't want to stay in remand. The conditions there are bad—not enough food and many kids get scabies. In adult remand prison it's even worse. They plead guilty because they want to get out faster. Then when we meet with them to prepare the pre-sentencing report they tell us of extenuating circumstances or say that they didn't do it.[172]

Six out of forty children we interviewed, who had been brought to court, told us that they pled guilty because they did not want to stay in remand. Some had been advised by cell mates to plead guilty. "My cell mates at the police station told me to say I had done it, or else I would be sent to Kodiaga [adult remand prison]. So when I was brought to court, I pled guilty and the magistrate sentenced me right there to borstal institution," said Brian, who had just been released from Shikusa Borstal Institution.[173]

Even if a child pleads guilty, however, the proceedings are not always expeditious. For example, fourteen-year-old Simon, who sleeps in a roundabout[174] in Nairobi, told us:

The magistrate asked me if I stole the light and I said yes. I said yes because I thought I'd be released faster. Then the magistrate said they needed to find the complainant [the person whose light had been stolen], and they sent me to Industrial Area Remand [for adults]. I stayed there from May to September, and was just released this month. I got twelve strokes with a plastic stick, on the back sides of my legs, and was made to wash the rooms in the court building.[175]

---

[172] Interview with probation officers of the Juvenile Law Court.

[173] Human Rights Watch interview with Brian, Kisumu, September 20, 1996.

[174] A roundabout is a circular road around a traffic island or park at the intersection of several major roads, around which motor vehicles circulate. Street children in Nairobi often sleep in roundabouts at night.

[175] Interview with Andrew, Nairobi, September 17, 1996.

He spent four months in adult remand, after pleading guilty to theft, awaiting sentence.

Further, once the magistrate orders correctional measures to be taken, they are not always immediately executed. During the interim period between sentencing and execution of the sentence, children are detained in police station lockups or on remand, waiting. For example, a child could spend weeks or even months in remand waiting for transport back home or for a parent to come and collect the child.[176] "And they don't get to reappear in court again, because they've already been sentenced," commented a representative of an NGO that works with street children in Nairobi;[177] thus their cases could go unmonitored by courts for months.

The practice of detaining street children in remand for unlimited periods of time contravenes established principles of international law which require that pre-trial detention be used only as a last resort and for the minimum period necessary.[178] The harmful effects of remanding children to institutions where they are mixed with criminal offenders and sometimes adult criminal offenders is magnified by the abusive conditions inside, particularly in adult remand prisons. Conditions in remand centers will be discussed below in Section VI of this report (on conditions in institutions).

Disposition of Cases: Sentencing

International law and standards provides basic guidelines on the adjudication and disposition of children's cases. The Beijing Rules require that courts investigate and consider the child's background and circumstances (in the form of a social inquiry report) before rendering a final disposition prior to sentencing, and that "[d]eprivation of personal liberty shall not be imposed unless the juvenile is adjudicated of a serious act involving violence against another person or of persistence in committing other serious offenses and unless there is no

---

[176] They also can wait weeks before arrangements are made for them to enter an approved school or a borstal institution to which the court has ordered they be committed.

[177] Human Rights Watch interview with NGO representative, Nairobi, September 19, 1996, anonymity requested.

[178] *See* Beijing Rules, Rule 13; U.N. Rules for the Protection of Juveniles, Rule 17.

other appropriate response."[179] Restrictions on the personal liberty of children shall be imposed only after careful consideration and for the minimum period necessary.[180] The Convention on the Rights of the Child calls for the use of a variety of alternatives to institutional care "to ensure that children are dealt with in a manner appropriate to their well-being and proportionate both to their circumstances and the offence."[181]

Kenyan law provides for a variety of correctional measures, including alternatives to institutional care. The juvenile court is authorized to dispose of a "protection or discipline" (P&C or P&D) case by ordering: release to a parent or guardian (either directly or through a repatriation order), committal to the care of a fit person or an approved voluntary institution, placement under the supervision of an approved officer or a children's officer, or committal to an approved school.[182] The juvenile court is authorized to dispose of a criminal case by ordering: discharge, probation, corporal punishment,[183] payment of a fine or compensation, committal to the care of a fit person or an approved voluntary institution or approved society,[184] committal to an approved school (if the child is fifteen years old or younger), committal to a borstal institution (if the child is fifteen years old or older), or committal to an adult prison (if the child is at least fourteen years old).[185] Again, there is an overlap between criminal and

---

[179] Beijing Rules, Rules 16.1 and 17.1(c).

[180] Ibid., Rule 17.1(b).

[181] Convention on the Rights of the Child, Article 40(4).

[182] Children and Young Persons Act, Article 25.

[183] International standards forbid the use of corporal punishment on children. Beijing Rules, Rule 17.3. Under Article 27(9) of the Penal Code of Kenya, corporal punishment "shall be inflicted with a rod, cane or other instrument of a type approved for the purpose by the Minister [of Home Affairs], and the Minister may approve different types of rod, cane or other instrument for different ages of persons."

[184] An approved voluntary institution, or approved society, is a body which works for the care, protection and control of children under the age of eighteen, and which must be approved for that purpose by the minister of home affairs. Children and Young Persons Act, Article 63.

[185] Children and Young Persons Act, Article 17.

"protection or discipline" cases in that children from either category may be committed to approved schools.

Magistrates have been criticized for their overuse of institutionalization as a correctional measure for children. In a 1995 report issued by ANPPCAN Kenya, a prominent children's NGO, it was stated:

> Whereas Section 17 of the Children and Young Persons Act provides for a whole range of penalties for children convicted of offences under the Act, the magistrates tend to overuse the penalty of institutionalization (sending the offenders to approved schools). These schools are few in number and offer conditions that are not always conducive to the rehabilitation of children. The schools were set up with the aim of rehabilitating the children back to normal social life, but they are said to be run on principles that have little room for the welfare of the child, and as a result they have failed to rehabilitate a large number of children admitted there. Indeed, some of the children are said to have run away from those schools and back to the streets, where they feel safer.[186]

Out of the forty children we interviewed who had appeared in court, twenty-two were ordered to be deprived of their liberty as punishment; twelve were committed to approved schools; three were committed to borstal institutions; and seven were committed to adult prisons (five of the seven were girls who were committed to Langata prison for women). The other eighteen children had their cases disposed of as follows: four were released; five were ordered to be repatriated back to their families in their home villages; one was released with a fine; two were given strokes and released; and six had not yet been sentenced and were still on remand.

The sentence and its duration are determined by the magistrate, usually following the recommendation of the children's officer or the probation officer in their investigation or pre-sentencing report. The period of committal to approved schools may extend up until a child reaches the age of eighteen.[187] However, children may sometimes stay in an approved school until they reach twenty years of age, in order to complete their education and sit for exams. We were told by the

---

[186] ANPPCAN, *Hearing on Street Children in Kenya*, p. 34.

[187] Children and Young Persons Act, Article 31(4).

manager of Likoni Approved School that almost all the boys there are "from the streets" and "most are about thirteen or fourteen years old when they come, and usually stay until they turn eighteen."[188] The deputy manager of Kirigiti Approved School also told us that most girls there stay until they turn eighteen.[189] Committals to borstal institutions are always for three years.[190]

Although consideration of a "social inquiry report" is normally required for the judicious adjudication and disposition of a case, we found that magistrates sometimes order correctional measures on the spot without consideration of an investigation or presentencing report. We observed this in the Juvenile Law Court in Nairobi and were told the same by children we interviewed. Upon pleading guilty to minor offenses, magistrates sometimes immediately ordered that children receive a number of cane strokes, or ordered them to perform chores around the court house (extra-mural penal employment) before being released. With backlogged and overburdened case loads, the summary disposition of cases involving minor offenses can be appropriate, in the interest of sparing children lengthy detentions on remand and in the interest of conserving judicial resources.[191] However, it is wholly inappropriate where the correctional measure ordered is deprivation of liberty or corporal punishment.

We found that it is not unusual for magistrates to order the deprivation of liberty (committal to an approved school or borstal institution or even a prison) without consideration of a pre-sentencing report. This happens most frequently in the cases of children who are tried in regular courts where they are mixed with adults. For example, four girls told us that they had each been arrested and taken to regular courts in Nairobi, where the magistrates sentenced them on the spot to Langata prison for women after they pled guilty to charges of "loitering with intent to solicit." Three of the girls were fourteen or fifteen years old at the time of

---

[188] Human Rights Watch interview with Justus Muthoka, manager of Likoni Approved School, September 27, 1996.

[189] Human Rights Watch interview with Sophia Gikanga, deputy manager of Kirigiti Approved School, September 25, 1996.

[190] Boys may be released on probation, "discharged on license," after the first year of the three-year sentence. Borstal Institutions Act, Articles 6(1), and 26(1).

[191] *See also* Beijing Rules, Rule 16.1.

arrest.[192] Masi, after spending three nights in lockup at Central Police Station, described her court hearing:

> From the police station, we were taken to City Court. The other two girls and me were the only kids there. The rest were all adults. The others in the cell advised me to plead guilty, because if I didn't, I'd be sent to remand. So when I got to court I pled guilty, and the magistrate said I was sentenced to Langata prison for one month.[193]

Seventeen-year-old Brian told us how he had been arrested in 1995, when he was sixteen. After spending one week in a crowded police cell in Kisumu police station, where he was caned by police, he was brought to court. He pled guilty to the charge of theft and was sentenced on the spot to three years in a borstal institution.[194] No consideration appears to have been given to the age of the children in these cases; they appear to have been tried as adult criminal offenders in regular courts with no regard for the special protections accorded to children—clearly, magistrates and police need to make greater efforts to ascertain the age of any young persons coming before them in their work to ensure that children are identified and dealt with accordingly.

---

[192] One of the girls did not know her age, but said that the police told her she was eighteen.

[193] Human Rights Watch interview with Masi, Nairobi, September 24, 1996.

[194] Human Rights Watch interview with Brian, Kisumu, September 20, 1996.

VI. CONDITIONS IN INSTITUTIONS TO WHICH CHILDREN ARE COMMITTED

When a person is taken into state custody, the government is obligated to meet certain minimum requirements under international law regarding the conditions under which the person is detained. The institutionalization of street children in Kenya fails on two counts. It fails to address the root of the problem which leads to the deluge of children on the streets, the economic and social hardships which lead children to take to the streets. It also fails as a remedial measure to provide children with the rehabilitation, support, and education required to enable them to live in the outside world as responsible and capable members of society. We found that the conditions in juvenile institutions in Kenya, to be discussed below, are often even counterproductive to these goals.

International Standards

Physical conditions

The U.N. Rules for the Protection of Juveniles set forth detailed specifications on the physical environment in which children can be confined. The U.N. Standard Minimum Rules for the Treatment of Prisoners does the same for prisoners generally; its application is extended "to the treatment of juvenile offenders in institutions" under Rule 27 of the Beijing Rules. These standards, although non-binding, have been recognized in the international community by adoption as General Assembly resolutions. They provide an authoritative statement of the international community's agreement on the minimum standards under which children may be confined by the state.

The U.N. Rules for the Protection of Juveniles state that children shall have the right to facilities and services that meet all the requirements of health and human dignity.[195] The facility's physical environment should be designed with the aim of rehabilitation and with due respect for the need of children for privacy, sensory stimuli, opportunities for association with peers and participation in sports, physical exercise and leisure time activities.[196] Every juvenile should be provided with sufficient bedding, which should be kept clean and in good order.[197] Sanitary

---

[195] U.N. Rules for the Protection of Juveniles, Rule 31.

[196] Ibid., Rule 32.

[197] Ibid., Rule 33.

installations should be of a sufficient standard to enable every juvenile to comply with his or her physical needs in privacy and in a clean and decent manner.[198] Children should have the right to use their own clothing, to the extent possible, and care should be taken to ensure that children have adequate clothing for the climate.[199] Suitably prepared food should be provided at regular meal times and should meet standards of dietetics, hygiene, and health.[200]

The U.N. Standard Minimum Rules for the Treatment of Prisoners similarly require that facilities provide adequate sleeping accommodation with due regard paid to the provision of sufficient bedding,[201] adequate sanitary installations,[202] bathing and shower installations,[203] toilet articles,[204] and regular meals of adequate nutritional value.[205]

Education and vocational training

The U.N. Rules for the Protection of Juveniles detail the parameters of the right to education, vocational training, and work for children deprived of their liberty.[206] Children of compulsory school age have the right to education which

---

[198] Ibid., Rule 34.

[199] Ibid., Rule 36.

[200] Ibid., Rule 37.

[201] U.N. Standard Minimum Rules for the Treatment of Prisoners, adopted Aug. 30, 1955 by the First United Nations Congress on the Prevention of Crime and the Treatment of Offenders, U.N. Doc. A/CONF/611, annex I, E.S.C. res. 663C, 24 U.N. ESCOR Supp. (No. 1) at 11, U.N. Doc. E/3048 (1957), amended E.S.C. res. 2076, 62 U.N. ESCOR Supp. (No. 1) at 35, U.N. Doc. E/5988 (1977), Rule 19.

[202] Ibid., Rule 12.

[203] Ibid., Rule 13.

[204] Ibid., Rule 15.

[205] Ibid., Rule 20(1).

[206] *See* U.N. Rules for the Protection of Juveniles, Rules 38-46.

should be "designed to prepare him or her for return to society."[207] Juveniles above compulsory school age who wish to continue their education should be permitted and encouraged to do so, and every effort should be made to provide them with access to appropriate educational programs.[208] Although education is not yet compulsory in Kenya, the Kenyan government has committed itself to providing tuition-free education at the primary level (standards 1-8) to all. That commitment should also extend to children who are deprived of their liberty by the state, with an additional commitment to provide them with books and study materials.

Children deprived of their liberty have the right to receive vocational training in occupations likely to prepare them for future employment,[209] and those who work should receive equitable remuneration for their labor.[210] The Beijing Rules state that the objectives of institutional treatment of children are to provide education and vocational skills "with a view to assisting them to assume socially constructive and productive roles in society"[211] and "with a view to ensuring that they do not leave the institution at an educational disadvantage."[212]

Discipline and punishment

As mentioned earlier, international law is clear and consistent in its prohibition of torture and inhuman or degrading treatment of children. The Convention on the Rights of the Child states that children deprived of their liberty "shall be treated with humanity and respect for the inherent dignity of the human person" and that no child "shall be subjected to torture or other cruel, inhuman or degrading treatment or punishment."[213] The Beijing Rules provide that "[j]uveniles

---

[207] Ibid., Rule 38.

[208] Ibid., Rule 39.

[209] Ibid., Rule 42.

[210] Ibid., Rule 46.

[211] Beijing Rules, Rule 26.1.

[212] Ibid., Rule 26.6.

[213] Convention on the Rights of the Child, Article 37.

shall not be subject to corporal punishment."[214] The U.N. Rules for the Protection of Juveniles prohibit the use of restraints or force on children unless all other control methods have been exhausted and failed,[215] and prohibit all disciplinary measures constituting cruel, inhuman or degrading treatment, "including corporal punishment, placement in a dark cell, closed or solitary confinement or any other punishment that may compromise the physical or mental health of the juvenile concerned."[216] They explicitly prohibit "the reduction of diet and the restriction or denial of contact with family members" for any purpose, and the use of labor as a disciplinary sanction.[217]

Grievance procedures

The U.N. Rules for the Protection of Juveniles require that, upon admission to a detention facility, all children be given a copy of the institution's governing rules and a written description of their rights and obligations so that children may understand, among other aspects of their confinement, the disciplinary requirements and procedures of the institution and the mechanisms by which they can raise complaints to competent authorities.[218] They further require that children be allowed to make uncensored complaints to the institution's director, central administration, or any other proper authorities, and be informed of the response without delay.[219]

Remand Institutions

Juvenile Remand Homes

Juvenile remand homes, established under Article 36 of the Children and Young Persons Act, are under the administration of the Children's Department, which also oversees the running of approved schools. There are eleven such homes

---

[214] Beijing Rules, Rule 17.3.

[215] U.N. Rules for the Protection of Juveniles, Rules 63-64.

[216] Ibid., Rule 67.

[217] Ibid.

[218] Ibid., Rules 24-25.

[219] Ibid., Rules 75-76.

Conditions in Institutions to Which Children Are Commited 75

in Kenya, with a reported total capacity of 2,500 children.[220] The three most common legal bases for the detention of children in juvenile remand homes are: "destitution and vagrancy" (1,800); "beyond parental control" (500); and "found begging" (480).[221] The overwhelming majority of the population in juvenile remand homes is comprised of street children. Staff at Nairobi Juvenile Remand Home, told us that "90 percent of the kids are here because of vagrancy."[222] No efforts are made to separate children by the severity of their offenses, or to separate children accused or convicted of criminal offenses from children "in need of protection or discipline." This practice contravenes international standards which require that "[u]ntried detainees should be separated from convicted juveniles"[223] and may have criminalizing effects on children.

---

[220] Materials provided to Human Rights Watch by the Children's Department on December 18, 1996, on file with Human Rights Watch ("Children's Department Materials"), p. 3. The names and locations of Juvenile Remand Homes are as follow: Nairobi (in Nairobi, Nairobi Province), Eldoret (in Eldoret, Rift Valley Province), Nyeri (in Nyeri, Central Province), Likoni (in Mombasa, Coast Province), Malindi (in Kilifi, Coast Province), Kisumu (in Kisumu, Nyanza Province), Kericho (in Kericho, Rift Valley Province), Murang'a (in Murang'a, Central Province), Kiambu (in Kiambu, Central Province), Nakuru (in Nakuru, Rift Valley Province), and Kakamega (in Kakamega, Western Province).

In addition to the eleven remand homes, the Children's' Department oversees one Government Children's Home in Nairobi, for children under eight years old. It can take up to eighty children and is the only one of its kind in Kenya. Report of Ministry of Home Affairs and National Heritage, Children's Department, October 1996, on file with Human Rights Watch, p.7.

[221] These figures are as of October 1, 1996 and are representative of long-term trends; out of 98,204 "cases handled by Children's Department" between 1964 and 1996, the three most common cases were "destitution and vagrancy" (52,048), "beyond parental and guardian control" (14,730), and "found begging or receiving alms" (13,748). Children's Department Materials, p. 4.

[222] Interview with staff of Nairobi Juvenile Remand Home.

[223] U.N. Rules for the Protection of Juveniles, Rule 17.

The Children's Department has issued internal rules and regulations "for the good administration of children's institutions throughout the country."[224] These regulations require, among other things, that the manager of any children's institution keep detailed records of all committals of children to the institution, including an admission and discharge register, daily log book, punishment register, and individual case files for each child (Regulation 2). Records must be available for inspection at all times by children's officers or other authorized persons, who may inspect the institutions with or without notice. Parents or guardians may be granted reasonable access to visit and communicate with children (Regulation 3). Corporal punishment should be avoided, particularly for children under the age of seven, "unless absolutely necessary and should be administered by the manager and recorded in the corporal punishment register" (Regulation 6). The rules and regulations also call for the provision of adequate space to accommodate the children, separate beds and bedding for each child, adequate sanitary installations, "water supply to be ensured all the time," a balanced diet, and arrangements for the educational and recreational needs of each child.[225]

Conditions in remand centers vary but generally suffer from common problems of run-down facilities, inadequate supplies of water and inoperative sanitary installations, inadequate and dirty bedding materials, the frequent use of corporal punishment and no provisions whatsoever for the recreational and educational needs of children. Overcrowding was found to be severe in Nairobi Juvenile Remand Home.

We visited Nairobi Juvenile Remand Home (Kabete) on October 4, 1996, with the permission of the Children's Department. On the day of our visit, 153 children (125 boys and twenty-eight girls) were present in the home. Staff stated

---

[224] Important Information on Rules and Regulations from Children's Department Office, Nairobi, August 16, 1995 ("Children's Department Regulations"), on file with Human Rights Watch.

[225] Children's Department Regulations, Section II (Basic Requirements). Regarding education and recreation, the regulations state:
1. Each child's educational needs should be assessed on admission. Arrangements should thereafter be made for suitable classroom instruction to be given either on or off the premises.
2. Religious instructions according to each child's religious persuasion should be made available.
3. Being a child's right, recreation is important for mental, physical and social growth and development. Children should be allowed ample time for games, sports, etc. Equipment and grounds for this should be safe from sharp objects.

that the capacity of the home is eighty.[226] They told us that, "sometimes the number goes up to around 500, like in mid-September, because of police roundups."[227] The children ranged in age from seven to sixteen. There were four dormitories, three for boys (divided by age) and one for girls. The buildings were arranged around a courtyard in which the children take their meals. According to staff, children are given porridge in the morning and sometimes bread. Lunch consists of rice with beans or another vegetable, and *ugali* and beans for dinner. The dorms contained rows of bunk beds, with mattresses, and usually a blanket for each bed. Some beds had no blankets, and none had pillows or sheets. Children we interviewed on the street who had been confined there, said they had to share beds, sleeping two to a bed, and that mattresses were dirty and "blankets were infested with lice and bedbugs."[228] The dorms had grilled windows on one wall; ventilation was poor and the rooms smelled of body odor. Attached to the girl's dorm was an "ablutions area," which contained three squat toilet stalls, shower stalls, and two sinks. One of the sinks was filled to the brim with brown water and appeared to be clogged. When the faucet was turned on, no water came out. The toilets were backed up and clogged with excrement. In the "ablutions area" attached to the dorm for middle-aged boys, both sinks were missing from the base. Children we interviewed on the streets who had been confined there complained of constipation, scabies, and lack of water.

We visited Likoni Juvenile Remand Home, near Mombasa, on September 27, 1996 with the permission of the Children's Department. The remand home is located on the same grounds as Likoni Approved School. The remand home consists of two barn-like corrugated tin structures, one for boys and one for girls. According to the staff, there were twenty-two children staying in the remand home when we visited.[229] The girls' room was very dark and had only one window. The

---

[226] In materials provided to us by the Children's Department, the stated capacity of Nairobi Juvenile Remand Home (Kabete) is 600. Children's Department Materials, p. 3. We find the stated capacities of Kabete (600), Likoni (100) and Kisumu (220) Juvenile Remand Home (all visited by Human Rights Watch) to be gross overestimates of the capacities of these institutions.

[227] Interview with staff of Nairobi Juvenile Remand Home.

[228] Human Rights Watch interview with Alfred, Kisumu, September 21, 1996.

[229] According to the Children's Department, the capacity of the remand home is 100. Children's Department Materials, p. 3.

ventilation was extremely poor. There were a few foam mattresses pushed together on the floor in the middle of the room with some blankets strewn on top, on which all the girls slept together. There was an attached bathroom which was so poorly lit that we could not make out its interior. It appeared to be a hall with two dark stalls, and a large metal drum containing hauled water. The boys' room was larger, but equally dark and poorly ventilated. There was a stack of foam mattresses in the rear of the room, with a pile of blankets, that are brought out at night for the boys to sleep on. Aside from the bedding materials, both rooms were completely bare. The children receive their meals from the approved school, located nearby, but do not mix with the children there.

More disturbing than the physical conditions in which children are confined, was the complete absence of any educational or recreational activity for children, the deprivation of which has aggravated effects when children are held in remand for long periods of time. As stated earlier, some children can stay in remand for years without so much as a book or a ball to provide them with stimulation. In all three remand homes we visited (Nairobi, Likoni, and Kisumu),[230] the schedule of the children was the same. Children rise in the early morning, perform chores and eat porridge. They then stay in the compound, usually in an enclosed courtyard or in their dorms, until lunch is served at noon. After lunch they are usually locked in their dorms again until dinner is served at around 6:00 p.m. After dinner they are locked in for the night. There are no activities for the children throughout the day, educational or recreational, aside from an occasional visit from NGO volunteers who provide the children with a brief respite from the tedium of the day.

At Nairobi Juvenile Remand Home (Kabete), although we were told by staff that children are free to play outside in the courtyard, we observed during our visit that the grounds were eerily silent and that there were no children in sight. We observed through the dormitory windows that all the children were in their dorms, lying on their beds (two children per bed), with the doors shut and locked from the outside. When we asked staff why the children were not free to play in the enclosed courtyard, they responded that the children wanted to stay inside. One of the boys who we interviewed on the streets who had been confined there,

---

[230] We unofficially visited Kisumu Juvenile Remand Home on September 21, 1996. According to staff, there were sixty-six children (fifty boys and sixteen girls) there on the day of our visit. According to the Children's Department, the capacity of the remand home is 220. Children's Department Materials, p. 3.

explained, "unless we're working or eating, we're locked in the dorm."[231] In Kisumu Juvenile Remand Home, children also reported that they spent their days shut in their dorms, except when working or eating:

> We would rise at about 5 a.m., and do exercises and chores, like cleaning the rooms and the toilets. Then we'd have breakfast at 7 a.m. Then we'd have to go back in the dorm and stay inside until lunch. Some kids would be selected out to go work on the farm, cutting grass and digging. The older boy leaders, the ones who had been there a long time, decided which kids would have to work on the farm. At noon, we were allowed out of the dorm and given lunch, and then shut inside again until supper.[232]

Similarly, in Likoni Juvenile Remand Home, fifteen-year-old Mugambi told us he had no complaints "but there's nothing to do all day except go and haul water."[233] At the time of our interview, he had been in remand for three years.

Further, children said that they are beaten or caned by staff if they misbehave or fight with other children. One boy we interviewed said he had been beaten by staff on a daily basis while in Nairobi Juvenile Remand, "with a strip of rubber from a tire."[234] Another boy who had been confined in Likoni said a few boys that tried to escape were beaten by five teachers from the attached approved school while he was there.[235] Fifteen-year-old Alfred, who was remanded in Kisumu Juvenile Remand in June 1996 described being caned not by staff, but by senior boys at the remand home who appear to play a supervisory role for other children.[236]

---

[231] Human Rights Watch interview with Peter, Nairobi, September 17, 1996.

[232] Human Rights Watch interview with Alfred, Kisumu, September 21, 1996.

[233] Human Rights Watch interview with Mugambi, Likoni Juvenile Remand Home, September 27, 1996.

[234] Human Rights Watch interview with Peter, Mombasa, September 28, 1996.

[235] Human Rights Watch interview with Tom, Mombasa, September 28, 1996.

[236] Human Rights Watch interview with Alfred, Kisumu, September 21, 1996.

Adult Remand Prisons

Under Kenyan law children fourteen years old and above may be remanded to adult remand prisons, "where they must be kept separate from the adults."[237] Remanding children to adult facilities happens all too frequently; nine out of thirty-five children we interviewed who were committed to remand institutions were sent to adult remand prisons. The youngest was twelve years old. In contravention of international law, the children are often commingled with adults in the remand prisons. More important, conditions in adult remand, whether in a separate children's section or mixed with adults, are extremely abusive. The atmosphere is penal. Unlike juvenile remand homes, which are under the administration of the Children's Department, remand prisons are under the administration of the Prisons Department.[238] Children there face serious problems of overcrowding, unsanitary conditions, hunger, and physical abuse far worse than in juvenile remand homes.

The U.S. Department of State's report on human rights in Kenya for 1996 summarized conditions in prison, including remand, as follows:

> Prison conditions are at times life threatening, due in part to lack of resources, and in part to the Government's unwillingness to address deficiencies in the penal system. Prisoners are subjected to severe overcrowding, inadequate water, poor diet, substandard bedding, and deficient health care. In October 1995, Justice Emmanuel O'kubasu stated that Kenyan prisons are "death chambers." The same month, Home Affairs Minister Francis Lotodo reported that 814 prisoners had died in jails in the first 9 months of 1995, due chiefly to dysentery and diarrhea. As of August 1994, Kenya's 78 prisons held a daily average of 39,000

---

[237] Interview with former magistrate of the Juvenile Law Court.

[238] Remand prisons are regulated under the Prisons Act (Chapter 90 of the Laws of Kenya), and the Prisons Rules (subsidiary legislation under Section 74 of the Prisons Act.) The Prisons Act and Prisons Rules set forth basic requirements concerning all aspects of the treatment of prisoners, including the physical conditions of their imprisonment, health care, discipline and punishment of prisoners, and discipline and punishment of prison officers for misconduct. Prisoners on remand fall in the "unconvicted prisoner" class. The only special provision found for children who are in remand prison, is that corporal punishment "shall be limited to ten strokes in the case of persons of or under the apparent age of sixteen years." (Article 55(1)).

inmates, 12,000 of whom were awaiting trial. Some facilities such as the Nairobi Remand Prison, are overcrowded by several hundred percent. Rape of both male and female inmates is a serious problem, as is the growing incidence of AIDS. Prisons do not have resident doctors, and only one prison had a doctor permanently assigned. . . .Officially, there is separate confinement for men, women, and children. However, there are cases in which men and women have been put in the same cells, and youths (as young as early teenagers) are frequently kept in cells with adults in overcrowded prisons and remand centers. The Government does not permit independent monitoring of prison conditions.[239]

Although we were not permitted by the Prisons Department to visit any remand prisons, we were able to interview children on the streets who had been detained in four remand prisons: Industrial Area (in Nairobi), Shimolatewa (in Mombasa), Kodiaga (in Kisumu), and Langata (for women, in Nairobi).

Children reported that conditions in Industrial Area Remand were particularly severe. In December 1994, Minister of Home Affairs Francis Lotodo stated that there were 583 deaths in Nairobi Industrial Area Remand Prison in the preceding four years,[240] yet children continue to be remanded to this facility. Children told us they slept on the floor, without mattresses, in extremely crowded rooms. A few had blankets, which they said were filthy and lice infested. Toilets were overflowing and made the rooms stink. Drinking water was available in very limited quantities, and bathing facilities were nonexistent. Sixteen-year-old William described physical conditions in Industrial Area's section for boys, as follows:

> There was a toilet in the room, but no water. There were eighty-seven of us in the room. The room smelled, and there were bugs and lice, bedbugs, cockroaches and even rats. We had some

---

[239] U.S. Department of State, Kenya Country Report on Human Rights Practices for 1996, Section 1(c). *See generally*, Kenya Human Rights Commission Prisons Project, *A Death Sentence: Prisons Conditions in Kenya*, (Kenya: Kenya Human Rights Commission, 1996).

[240] Kenya Human Rights Commission Prisons Project, *A Death Sentence: Prison Conditions in Kenya*, p. 79.

> blankets, but no mattress or beds. It was so crowded, I had to sleep outside the room, by the toilet, sitting up. After a week, [the inmates] let me sleep in the room, on my side because there wasn't enough room to lie on your back. The windows were barred, and there were lights on in the cell which they kept on while you slept. They brought us one bucket of water at night for all the boys.[241]

Similarly disturbing conditions were described in Kodiaga remand:

> There were four cell blocks. I was in block C with about twenty-five other boys. There were no windows, but there were vents at the tops of the walls. There was nothing in the room, aside from a few rags to sleep with. There was a toilet, but no running water. They brought us water to drink, but not enough. Everyone was filthy. There was no water to wash with and no soap either. There was a cement ditch filled with water that they allowed us to bathe in once a month. That water was so filthy, I preferred not to bathe at all.[242]

Boys consistently complained that there was not enough food, and that older boys or adults would sometimes snatch away what little food they were given. Even where children are separated from adults, they might still overlap during meals. "For lunch, the B and C blocks were mixed together, so we were mixed with adults then. Some of the men would steal some kids's food," said William, who was in Industrial Area for four weeks on vagrancy charges.[243] According to the children, meals consist of a thin porridge in the early morning, followed by a small portion of ugali and beans for lunch at around 10:30 a.m., and an early supper at around 3:00 p.m. From 3:00 p.m. until the next morning children were given nothing more to eat and complained about hunger especially during this period.

In addition to grossly inadequate physical conditions, boys complained of physical and sexual abuse and harassment by other inmates. For example, boys

---

[241] Human Rights Watch interview with William, Nairobi, October 2, 1996.

[242] Human Rights Watch interview with Simon, Mombasa, September 28, 1996.

[243] Human Rights Watch interview with William, Nairobi, October 2, 1996.

who had been remanded in Industrial Area said that older boys, who had been there for long periods of time, played a supervisory and authoritarian role over the other children, who live at the whim and mercy of these internal rulers of the remand cells. Robert, who had been confined in Industrial Area Remand, described the abusive treatment that children suffer at the hands of other inmates:

> There were two older boys in the room who supervised everyone. They might beat you up, or sell your clothes to buy cigarettes, or take your food. One of them tried to seduce me, but I refused, so I was beaten up and had my clothes taken away from me. They smeared excrement from the toilet all over my body. I tried to complain to the prison guards about it, but they wouldn't listen. I had to stay in my underwear until a friend of mine came to visit me and brought me some clothes. The next time I went to court, I pled guilty, because I didn't want to have to go back there.[244]

Children repeatedly said that guards were indifferent to their needs and complaints -- that prison guards did not respond to requests for water, complaints of illness, or complaints about abuse from other inmates. One boy said that prison guards were even "paid off" by the older boys who were the "leaders."[245]

Not only do the guards do nothing to assist the children, but in Shimolatewa, Kodiaga and Industrial Area, children complained of physical abuse by guards themselves. "I got along fine with the other boys and the men, but the guards beat us all the time. Sometimes they'd use a *rungu* [baton], and they'd hit us aiming for the joints. I still feel the pain in my knees from the *rungu*," said sixteen-year-old James, who was detained in Shimolatewa remand prison in April 1996.[246] Boys in Industrial Area said they had been beaten by guards with whips, and also with batons aimed at their joints.[247] One boy who had been remanded in Kodiaga for six weeks described being beaten indiscriminately by prison guards:

---

[244] Human Rights Watch interview with Robert, Nairobi, September 30, 1996.

[245] Human Rights Watch interview with Mwangi, Nairobi, September 26, 1996.

[246] Human Rights Watch interview with James, Likoni Juvenile Remand Home, September 27, 1996.

[247] Human Rights Watch interview with William, Nairobi, October 2, 1996.

"seven guards came bursting into the room and were beating us all for no reason. Then they ordered us all to strip and to go outside to the courtyard, where they made us jump up and down for half an hour. Some of the people were sick and weak, and couldn't jump, so the guards beat them and kicked them."[248]

The two girls we interviewed (aged twelve and fourteen), who had been remanded in 1995 to Langata Remand Prison, said they were not mistreated by guards or inmates there. Unlike the remand prisons for men, the girls were given mattresses and blankets. The twelve-year-old said she and other young girls were kept separately from the adult women. The fourteen-year-old said she was held with adults.[249]

Finally, as in juvenile remand facilities, adult remand prisons offer no activities for the children whatsoever. Children consistently said they were shut in their rooms or cells all day, except for meal times and a brief period outside in the morning. Several children remarked in separate interviews that the only pastime in remand prisons is "killing the lice."

Approved Schools

After spending periods of varying length on remand, children may be committed by courts to approved schools, established under Article 37 of the Children and Young Persons Act. Like juvenile remand homes, approved schools are under the administration of the Children's Department and are subject to the same internal regulations. We found that conditions in approved schools were generally better than in the remand centers. Most importantly, children receive education and/or vocational training up to a certain level in approved schools, although the quality of that education has been criticized by NGOs. A principal criticism of approved schools is that children from many different backgrounds, and sent to the schools for diverse reasons, are mixed together; serious offenders may negatively influence other children who are there simply because they are homeless, abandoned, or orphaned. Although approved schools are supposedly aimed at educating and rehabilitating children for return to society, "the approved

---

[248] Human Rights Watch interview with Simon, Mombasa, September 28, 1996. The described practice appears to be a means of searching inmates for concealed items.

[249] Human Rights Watch interview with Susan, Nairobi, October 2, 1996; Human Rights Watch interview with Victoria, Nairobi, October 2, 1996.

school's reputation for being little more than a prison means it is difficult for the inmates to find employment [and acceptance] when they are released."[250]

Mixing of Children

There are eleven approved schools in Kenya: one for the reception and distribution of children to other approved schools, four for children in need of "protection and care", and six for children in need of "protection and discipline."[251] According to the Children's Department, "[t]he P&C category handles and rehabilitates [children] who are non-offenders but lack responsible parenthood, homeless, and destitutes who require care, support, and protection. The other category (P&D) caters for Juvenile Delinquents and those beyond parental control."[252] The director of the Children's Department acknowledged that "the demarcation between P&C and P&D cases is very thin." As discussed earlier, the distinction between P&C and P&D cases is in many ways arbitrary. Further, approved schools designated for P&D children also receive children convicted of criminal offenses.

In practice children are often mixed together from all categories, P&C, P&D, and criminal offenders. A representative from an NGO that runs a street children's program in Nairobi said:

> The system of approved schools serves so many different purposes under one roof that it ends up being detrimental to all children. Lost children are mixed with criminal kids. Plus there are inadequate resources -- no activities for the children, poor quality in education, unmotivated staff and teachers, and the

---

[250] Munyakho, *Kenya: Child newcomers in the urban jungle*, p. 29.

[251] The approved school designated as a reception and distribution center is Gethathuru (in Nairobi). Schools designated for P&C cases are Othaya (in Nairobi), Thika (in Thika), Dagoretti (in Nairobi), and Machakos (in Machakos). Schools designated for P&D cases are Kabete (in Nairobi), Kakamega (in Kakamega), Kericho (in Kericho), Wamamu (in Kirinyaga), Likoni (in Mombasa), and Kirigiti (in Kiambu). Children's Department Materials, p. 1.

[252] Ibid.

punitive measures are too harsh, as if all the children are small criminals."[253]

Most children in approved schools are street children.[254]

According to the Children's Department, approved schools are also designated for children by age group: junior, medium, and senior.[255] However, in each of the three senior approved schools we visited (Kakamega, Likoni and Kirigiti), we found children of all ages.[256] Further, although the Children and Young Persons Act requires that children must be at least ten years old to be committed to an approved school unless the child "cannot be suitably dealt with otherwise,"[257] we found children as young as seven years old in one of the approved schools we visited (Kirigiti).

Physical Conditions
Overcrowding does not appear to be a problem, with the notable exception of Kirigiti (the only approved school for girls). In Kirigiti, there were 188 girls there on the day of our visit. According to the deputy manager of the school, the capacity of the school is 160.[258] Girls in Kirigiti are separated into different

---

[253] Human Rights Watch interview with NGO representative, Nairobi, October 1, 1996, anonymity requested.

[254] Interview with Director of Children's Department.

[255] Approved Schools for "junior" children are Thika, Dagoretti and Kericho. Schools for "medium" children are Othaya and Machakos. Schools for "senior" children are Kabete, Kakamega, Wamamu, Likoni, and Kirigiti. Children's Department Materials, pp. 1-2.

[256] With the permission of the Children's Department, we visited: Kakamega Approved School on September 23, 1996 and interviewed the manager, Mr. Litali; Likoni Approved School on September 27, 1996 and interviewed the manager, Justus Muthoka; and Kakamega Approved School on September 25, 1996 and interviewed the deputy manager, Sophia Gikanga.

[257] Children and Young Persons Act, Article 16(2).

[258] According to materials provided to us by the Children's Department, the capacity of Kirigiti Approved School is 300.

dormitories according to age, but in Likoni and Kakamega boys of all ages are mixed together in the dorms. According to the Children's Department, approved schools are operating under capacity, with 3,285 children registered in schools that reportedly have a combined capacity for holding 6,000 children.[259]

The physical surroundings in the schools were spartan, and parts of buildings were in disrepair. In Kirigiti, the dorms were spare, with metal frame bunk beds with mattresses covered by one blanket. Walls were chipped, peeling, and graffiti-scratched. Metal lockers in the dorms were battered and had been pried open. The concrete of the dining hall floor was torn up in sections and rough and uneven. In Kakamega, walls were similarly battered and peeling, and windows broken. Instead of mattresses, some bed frames were covered with rough burlap sacking. The dining hall had a few tables, but no benches. In Likoni, some bed frames were so misshapen that they resembled hammocks more than beds, with the centers of the beds sagging down to the floor. The schools appeared to have adequate sanitary installations for the children, although water shortages are all too frequent. Children had no complaints about the quality or quantity of the food.

Health facilities, where they exist, are minimal, although internal regulations require that a health officer be assigned to each approved school. Likoni Approved School had no nurse for the school. "If children are sick, we take them to the hospital in a vehicle," said the manager. At Kakamega, where there was a basic dispensary, the nurse told us that the children's most common ailments are "respiratory infections, malaria, and soft tissue injuries from playing too hard." When questioned about the existence of HIV and AIDS, the nurse said there were no such cases at the school.

Girls are particularly hard hit by shortages of material resources. The deputy manager of Kirigiti said, "when we have money, we'll try to give them panties, and cotton for when they menstruate, but we get the same funding as the boys get, and girls have more needs than boys." Children in approved schools are provided with two sets of uniforms and soap. Everything else, including toothpaste, toothbrushes, shoes, toilet paper, towels, and additional clothing must be provided by the child's family, if she or he has any.

Education and Vocational Training

The children's schedules in all three schools we visited were similar. Children generally rise in the early morning at around 6:15 a.m., perform house chores, and gather for breakfast and inspection. They then are dispersed to their classes where they stay until 10:30 a.m., when they have a half-hour recess,

---

[259] Children's Department Materials, pp. 1-2.

followed by more classes and then lunch at around 12:45 p.m. After lunch the children return to classes until 4:00 p.m. when they break for the day. They then have free time or participate in extracurricular activities. Dinner is served at around 6:00 p.m. after which children retire to their dorms for the night.

Most children in approved schools receive basic education, up to standard 8, following the national 8-4-4 syllabus. All children are supposed to take regular academic courses as well as vocational training classes. The managers of Likoni and Kakamega Approved Schools said that boys are given a choice in the type of vocational training they receive (masonry, tailoring, carpentry, leather work, agricultural training, or sign painting). Products made by the children are sold to the public, but the children are not compensated for their labor. In fact, at the time of our visits, children were busy preparing products for the Nairobi International Show, an annual international commerce and trade fair held.

We found that in Kirigiti, some older girls end up taking only vocational training and no regular academic subjects at all. The deputy manager said that "not all girls go to classes. Instead, some go to vocational training only -- dress making and tailoring, or housekeeping. These girls sit for trade tests at the end of the year." We interviewed one girl on the streets of Nairobi, who had been in Kirigiti for three years before escaping in 1995. She told us that she had not attended regular classes, but had done knitting for three years at Kirigiti, from age eleven to fourteen. She said that although she voluntarily chose to do knitting, older girls had no choice in the matter; "if you come in and you're an older girl, you have to do the vocational classes."[260]

Discriminatory effects are felt by girls who wish to pursue secondary level education in an approved school. Kabete Approved School (in Nairobi) is the only approved school which offers secondary level education. It is restricted to boys. Thus girls are unable to continue their education in approved school beyond standard 8.[261]

Discipline and Punishment

The principal complaint of children we interviewed was over the use of corporal punishment by staff. Managers of all three approved schools stressed that corporal punishment is discouraged and used only as a last resort for serious

---

[260] Human Rights Watch interview with Serena, Nairobi, September 24, 1996.

[261] The director of Children's Services informed us that a small fund is set aside to provide for tuition fees for qualified girls from Kirigiti to attend secondary schools. The fund, however, is extremely limited.

offenses such as running away or stealing. The manager of Kakamega told us that a doctor must certify that a child is fit to receive corporal punishment before it can be given, and that the punishment should be entered in a register. According to him, corporal punishment must be administered in the presence of the manager and a third person. If children have complaints about the punishment, or about anything else, they can complain to "section heads" or directly to the manager. "For all of this year, we have not received any complaints from children," he said. The deputy manager of Kirigiti told us that "caning is not encouraged, and it would have to be on the girls' palms, and no more than five strokes." According to the manager of Kakamaega, deprivation of meals and isolation or seclusion of children is also permissible but is not practiced.

Children told us that they were caned for offenses as minor as having buttons missing from a uniform, not doing homework, making noise, accidentally breaking a window pane, fighting with other children, "going to the gate of the school," and not returning from town on time. According to the children, the beatings were usually administered with wooden sticks by house masters, house mothers, teachers, and occasionally managers. One boy, who had been in Likoni Approved School, told us that "the teachers are much worse than the manager when it comes to the punishment—they hit you everywhere and kick you, and if you try to get up, they stamp on you."[262] In Kirigiti Approved School, we observed a teacher striking a child in class with a stick during a math lesson. One girl there described being beaten with a pipe on her buttocks, after attempting to run away.[263]

Children also reported non-corporal punishments including deprivation of town outings or home leave, and special chores such as cutting grass (slashing), digging, cutting firewood and cleaning offices. The deprivation of home leave and the imposition of hard labor, such as digging, contravenes international standards on the restriction of contact with family members for any purpose and on the use of labor as a disciplinary sanction.[264] Children are allowed home leave three times a year, during the spring, summer and winter, "on request and based on good

---

[262] Human Rights Watch interview with Peter, Mombasa, September 28, 1996.

[263] Human Rights Watch interview with Sarah, Kirigiti Approved School, September 25, 1996.

[264] U.N. Rules for the Protection of Juveniles, Rule 67.

discipline (reward)."[265] According to the deputy manager of Kirigiti, the punishment the children fear most is being denied home leave.

When a child is found to be a "persistent absconder, or is exercising a bad influence on the other inmates of the school," the Children and Young Persons Act authorizes the director of the Children's Department to apply to court for: a six-month increase in committal period (if the child is under sixteen years old); or for committal of the child to a borstal institution (if the child is over fifteen years old) or to a prison (if the child is at least fourteen) for the unexpired portion of the child's sentence.[266] However, no children we interviewed reported receiving this penalty. Staff at the schools also said that these measures are rarely used, if at all.

Schools are inspected by the provincial children's officer or the district children's officer of the Children's Department once every three months. The director of the Children's Department also told us that he personally inspects the schools, and speaks directly with children to find out if they have any problems; he said that since he took office in 1994 there has been no cause for disciplining staff for excessive use of force.

Borstal Institutions

Under Kenyan law, boys fifteen years old and above who are guilty of crimes as minor as vagrancy can be sent to a borstal institution for a period of three years for correction, education and vocational training. The borstal institutions system is governed by the Borstal Institutions Act. Like remand prisons, borstals

---

[265] Children's Department Materials, p. 1. A family member or guardian must come to the approved school to pick up the child and vouch for the child's return. Additionally, the manager of an approved school is authorized to grant children a "leave of absence" for such period and on such conditions as he or she deems fit (Children and Young Persons Act, Article 42). Children are allowed to receive visitors at any time, although few children have family who are able to travel the distances to come and visit them. Children must remain on the school grounds at all times, except if accompanied by a staff member, although at Likoni, the manager told us that "trustworthy"boys are allowed into town with the permission of the teacher on duty.

[266] Children and Young Persons Act, Article 46. Children may also be released early, "on license" to a parent or other fit person, at any time during the child's period of detention (Article 43). However, the manager of Kakamega told us that most children stay until they are eighteen, and that release on license is discouraged. The director of the Children's Department is also authorized to revoke the committal order of the court, and release a child unconditionally (Article 44).

are under the administration of the Prisons Department and are part of the penal system in Kenya. Borstals are staffed by borstal officers and prison officers who are accustomed to dealing with security for adult prisoners, and who have no special training for dealing with the special needs of children. Borstals are situated on larger prison grounds, in close proximity to adult prisons. Although separated from adult prisoners, boys see and pass adult prisoners while out working in the fields or on the common roads of the prison compound.

We were denied access to the only two borstal institutions in Kenya, Shimolatewa (in Mombasa, Coast Province) and Shikusa (in Kakamega, Western Province), but were able to interview three boys who had recently been released from both institutions. There are no borstal institutions for girls in Kenya. The boys' principal complaints concerned severe physical abuse by staff and other inmates, and the hard labor which inmates are made to perform. Additionally, academic education is only available for a select few, those in standards 7 and 8.

Mixing of Children

Boys are separated into dormitories according to the length of time spent in the borstal or by age, but never by the nature and severity of their underlying offenses. According to Robert, who spent one year in Shimolatewa before being released on probation in April 1996, new boys there (called "greys" or "stars") stay in a separate dorm, and after three months are transferred to one of two other dorms (where boys are called "blues").[267] According to Brian, who spent one year in Shikusa before being released on probation in June 1996, boys there are divided in the dorms into fifteen- to seventeen-year-olds and eighteen- to twenty-year-olds.[268] "Boys were there for things like *bhang* [marijuana], thefts, assault, robberies, even murder, and then there were boys like me who were innocent and hadn't done anything wrong -- all mixed together," he said. Boys said there were about 300 boys in each borstal. Further, although boys must be at least fifteen to be

---

[267] Human Rights Watch interview with Robert, Nairobi, September 30, 1996.

[268] Human Rights Watch interview with Brian, Kisumu, September 20, 1996. Borstal sentences are for three years always, and boys must be under eighteen at the time of sentencing. Thus the maximum permissible age of boys in Borstals is twenty; "no person shall be detained in a borstal institution after he has attained the age of twenty-one years." Borstal Institutions Act, Article 22(3).

committed to a borstal, children younger than fifteen are sometimes committed.[269] One of the three boys we interviewed was fourteen when he was committed to Shimolatewa.

Physical Conditions

Article 4 of the Borstal Institutions Act requires that every borstal institution shall provide "proper sanitary arrangements, water supply, food, clothing and bedding for the inmates thereof," and a "proper place for the reception of inmates who are ill." The Borstal Institutions Rules, under section 53 of the Borstal Institutions Act, provide further guidelines on the conditions under which children may be held there. All inmates shall be provided with clothing as the superintendent (the head of the borstal institution) directs, and with bedding materials adequate for warmth and health (Rules 32-33). Clothing shall be changed and washed at least weekly (Rule 34(1)). Every inmate shall be provided with a sufficient quantity of plain, wholesome food, in accordance with borstal "scales" (Rule 35).

Boys told us that they were given one uniform only (a pair of blue shorts and a blue shirt), upon admission into the borstal. If they wished to wash their uniform, they would have to stay without any clothes on while waiting for the uniform to dry. In Shikusa, Brian said that boys could bathe whenever they wanted to, but were not provided with soap or a towel. In Shimolatewa, boys said that running water was not available, and that only the boys who served as prefects were able to bathe regularly. Robert complained that in Shimolatewa, there were only three buckets for 300 boys, and that many boys had scabies as a result of not being able to bathe. Items such as toothpaste, toothbrushes, underwear, soap, towels and toilet paper must be provided by the boy's family or friends on the outside. In the dorms, boys had their own beds, but in Shimolatewa, "some beds had no mattresses, and some boys had to sleep just on the frames. There were no blankets. Mosquitoes were a problem."[270]

Boys from both borstals said that food was limited in quantity and poor in quality. They received porridge for breakfast, *ugali* and *sukuma wiki* for lunch, and *ugali* and beans for dinner. Seconds are never allowed. Robert complained that the beans were sometimes so undercooked and hard that he broke a tooth. In Shimolatewa, boys said that prefects used food to coerce boys into homosexual

---

[269] When mistakes are made regarding a boy's age, the boy must be brought to court for review of his case. Borstal Institutions Act, Article 22.

[270] Human Rights Watch interview with Robert, Nairobi, September 30, 1996.

activity. "They would give you their food, and then later on ask you, 'where's my food? I gave you my food, now you give me what I want.' They want sex, and if you don't give it to them, they beat you."[271] Also, boys called "cairos" are given extra food for cleaning out the toilets and "use the food they get to seduce hungry boys," said Robert.

According to the boys, both borstals have a medical officer attached to the institution. When boys fall ill they are transferred to a hospital for treatment. The reported treatment of children who are ill, as testified to below, is deplorable:

> I had a bad toothache and complained, but they did nothing. Finally, I pulled the tooth out. I also got TB when I was there and was taken to the hospital. I had to share a bed with no mattress with another person. There were six beds in the room. We were all handcuffed to the beds. There was a small bucket under the bed, which we could reach to go to the bathroom in. I stayed handcuffed to that bed for two months. They brought us food, but it was never enough and the beans were always undercooked and hard.[272]

Education and Vocational Training

Article 4 of the Borstal Institutions Act requires that every borstal institution shall provide "the means of giving such inmates educational, industrial, or agricultural training." In practice, borstals provide academic classes only for boys in standards seven and eight. According to the boys we interviewed, out of about 300 boys in each borstal only between twenty and thirty were assigned to the "school section." The rest receive no academic education at all, and instead labor all day long, unpaid. Upon receipt of a "work card" or "jail card," usually one month after admission into the borstal, boys begin their schedule. Those who are lucky enough to be placed in the "school section" attend academic classes, where they prepare for the KCPE exams. If they qualify, they might be transferred to Kabete Approved School (in Nairobi), where they may attend secondary school.

Boys who are assigned to a work section have no choice as to what vocation they will be trained in. William, who was in Shimolatewa for one year before being released in 1995, told us:

---

[271] Ibid.

[272] Ibid.

> I was put in the work section that took care of cows, which I didn't want to do. I asked if I could be switched to sign writing, but was told "this is a prison and you cannot do what you want to do." I never went to any regular classes. There were classes only for boys in standards 7 or 8. There were about ten boys in each of those classes. The rest of us worked. The only thing I learned at Shimolatewa was how to milk a cow.[273]

Even boys who are in the school section are also assigned vocational training (tailoring, carpentry, sign writing, brick making, and agricultural work). For example, Robert, who was placed in standard seven at Shimolatewa, was also assigned to work in the *shamba* (farm). No boys reported being paid for any work performed in the borstal.

In addition to their regular chores and vocational work, all boys are called on to perform *harambee* (the Kiswahili for "pulling together") on the borstal farms. At Shimolatewa, Robert described *harambee:*

> It happens whenever they need work done. When they call us, it can last up to a week. All but the sick must go. We go to the *shamba* and do digging, weeding, or planting. When you're working, the guards watch you with sticks, and beat you if you don't work hard enough. Even the prefect boys beat you if they want. The guards would tell us, 'dig like you're new tractors fresh from the factory.' You don't get any drinking water until you come back to eat. Your throat is so dry, you can't even spit.

At Shikusa, Brian described a similar practice:

> On weekends, all the boys must go to the *shamba* and work, unless you're sick, from eight in the morning until noon, lunchtime. The big boys watch over us with sticks. It's rough when you're new. You get beaten a lot. After lunch we would come back and be shut in the dorms until dinner.

A typical day for the boys, during the week, begins at 5:00 a.m. (at Shimolatewa) or 6:00 a.m. (at Shikusa). They do chores and exercises, and assemble for *kabba* (head count). After eating porridge, they break up into

---

[273] Human Rights Watch interview with William, Nairobi, October 2, 1996.

different sections and go to their classes. They break at 10:00 a.m. (at Shimolatewa) or noon (at Shikusa) for lunch, and then return to classes for three more hours. In the afternoon they retire to their dorms and rest. There are no recreational activities for the boys whatsoever. At around 6:00 p.m. they have dinner and are then locked into their dorms for the night.

Discipline and Punishment

The Borstal Institutions Rules provide detailed guidelines on the authorized disciplinary measures in borstal institutions. The enumerated Borstal Institution Offenses include: being idle, careless or negligent at work; making repeated and groundless complaints; any offense against good order and discipline; disobeying any order of the superintendent or of any other officer or any institution rule; and escape (Rule 50). In contravention of international law,[274] authorized punishments include: corporal punishment not to exceed ten strokes (which should be inflicted with a light cane on the buttocks); solitary confinement in a room for up to fourteen days; and restriction of diet for up to fifteen days, all upon medical certification that the child is fit to undergo such punishment (Rules 51-54, and Articles 32-37).[275] Under the Borstal Institutions Act, children are entitled to a hearing of the disciplinary charge against him, before being punished for any Borstal Institution Offense (Article 34). All punishments imposed on inmates must be recorded by the superintendent in a register (Article 38).

All three boys we spoke to complained about severe brutality inflicted on them and other boys by prison guards. They complained of frequent canings, and beatings with kicks and slaps. Robert described to us how he was beaten upon arrival at Shimolatewa by guards in the reception room: "In the reception room, there were some police [prison guards] and teachers, who beat me with batons, aiming at my joints. Some were kicking me. I don't know why they were beating me, as I had only just arrived."[276]

---

[274] As discussed earlier, international law expressly prohibits the use of corporal punishment, reduction in diet, and solitary confinement of children as punishment. *See* U.N. Rules for the Protection of Juveniles, Rule 67.

[275] The Borstal Institutions Act further provides for the deprivation of certain privileges for up to one month, including the privilege of "playing games," and the payment of earnings (Article 32). These punishments however are meaningless, as children told us they are not paid for their work and have no recreational activities.

[276] Human Rights Watch interview with Robert, Nairobi, September 30, 1996.

In contravention of international law,[277] isolation is used in both borstals as punishment. Brian described the use of isolation cells in Shikusa:

> There are twelve of them, located in the "recall block." The rooms are small, with one small window with metal bars. There's nothing in the room. They pour water on the floor so that you can't lie down and sleep. Every one who comes on duty canes you when you're in there. They let you out at night to get dinner, the only meal for the day. You are put in the recall block for doing things like selling your blanket to an *askari*, to get cigarettes.[278]

In Shimolatewa, the use of isolation rooms is similar:

> You're stripped of your clothing and put in the cell. They pour water on the floor, and give you only a half-ration of food once a day, but they give you plenty of water to drink. There's a bucket for a toilet, and you sleep on the floor. You stay there until the superintendent decides to let you out.[279]

Boys also described receiving non-corporal punishments such as orders to gather wood, clean dorms, and dig in the *shamba* (farm) for a number of days, despite international law's prohibition on the use of labor as a disciplinary sanction.[280] William said that he had been forced to dig in Shimolatewa's *shamba* for six weeks for fighting with another boy. The Borstal Institutions Rules also authorizes the superintendent to suspend the privilege of writing and receiving letters at any time for misconduct (Rule 42). It should be noted that every letter received or written by an inmate "shall be read by the superintendent" and may be stopped "on the grounds that [the superintendent] considers its contents are

---

[277] U.N. Rules for the Protection of Juveniles, Rule 67.

[278] Human Rights Watch interview with Brian, Kisumu, September 20, 1996.

[279] Human Rights Watch interview with Robert, Nairobi, September 30, 1996.

[280] U.N. Rules for the Protection of Juveniles, Rule 67.

Conditions in Institutions to Which Children Are Commited 97

objectionable or that it is of inordinate length" (Rule 45).[281] A boy also may be transferred from borstal to a regular prison to serve out the remainder of his sentence, if the commissioner of prisons finds the boy "is of such a character, or has conducted himself in such a manner, as to render his detention in such borstal institution to be no longer expedient."[282] An application to court must be made for the transfer and committal to prison.

In Shimolatewa, other cruel and brutal forms of punishment were described by both boys who had been confined there. They witnessed the use of public beatings, described by one of them as follows:

> The boy was stripped naked, and made to bend over a stand, shackled at the hands and ankles. They put a wet salted cloth on his back side, and give him strokes of a young supple bamboo cane. The other boys were assembled around to watch. This punishment was used for things like homosexual acts, or trying to escape, or smoking cigarettes or smoking *bhang*.[283]

William said that boys who are caught smoking are sometimes "made to eat the cigarettes and drink four liters of water, followed by seven days in the segregation room where you only get one meal a day." No boys described attending anything resembling a hearing before being punished. They said punishments were decided by teachers (prison guards) and sometimes by the superintendent.

Grievance Procedures

Under the Borstal Institutions Rules, upon admission to a borstal children must be informed of the rules concerning the disciplinary requirements of the institution and the methods of making complaints about conditions in the institutions (Rules 28-29). An inmate may make a request to any borstal staff

---

[281] It should be further noted here that the Borstal Institutions Rules place serious restrictions on the right of the child to communicate with the outside world. An inmate is entitled to write only one letter every week to persons who must be approved by the superintendent of the school, and to receive only one thirty-minute visit per month (of up to three persons at one time) (Rule 41). No home leave is allowed, although the commissioner of prisons may grant discretionary leaves of absence.

[282] Borstal Institutions Act, Article 42.

[283] Human Rights Watch interview with Robert, Nairobi, September 30, 1996.

member to see the commissioner of prisons or to see a member of the Board of Visitors (who is supposed to inspect borstals every month).[284] Such a request must be conveyed without delay to the superintendent, who is supposed to forward it to the commissioner or to the Board of Visitors (Rule 49). The superintendent must also make himself available to hear complaints of all inmates who have requested to see him (Rule 49).

In practice, boys said that they were informed of the rules of the borstal institutions at the time when they were given their "jail cards" or "work cards," a month after being admitted, but that they were not informed of any procedures for making complaints. They said attempts to complain about mistreatment by other boys or by guards are futile:

> You could complain, but the guards never help you, unless they catch the boy red handed. There was one boy called Boxer who tried to sodomize me, and I complained to the guards about it. They told me, 'it's been happening since prisons were made' and wouldn't do anything to help me.[285]

Boys said that in order to pass on a complaint to the superintendent of Shimolatewa, a written request had to be presented to the "welfare officer" of the borstal, who would forward the complaint to the superintendent. However, as Robert put it, "I had no paper or pen to make the complaint. I asked a guard for paper and a pen, and he said he would get it for me, but he never did, and I just gave up." He also said that boys could complain to the prison inspector during his visits, but that boys were afraid to do so because "once the inspector's gone, they'll beat you again, so you don't bother to complain.[286] There was a boy named Calvin

---

[284] The Board of Visitors is created under Article 20 of the Borstal Institutions Act, and is comprised of at least ten persons who are appointed by the minister of home affairs. A member of the After Care Committee of the Board of Visitors is supposed to visit the Borstal at least once a month for the purpose of hearing complaints of inmates, examining the punishment register, and ensuring that children are receiving proper care, education and training in the institution (Article 21).

[285] Human Rights Watch interview with Robert, Nairobi, September 30, 1996.

[286] The "prison inspector" referred to may have been a member of the Board of Visitors, or a children's officer.

who tried to complain about his punishment, and was afterwards beaten by the guards."

Discharge

As discussed earlier, boys are often discharged after serving the first year of a borstal sentence. Boys who are discharged early are given transportation money home, and are placed on probation for the remaining two years of their sentence. Director of Probation Services Joseph K. Gitau, who serves on the Board of Visitors for each borstal institution, said that around fifty boys are discharged early from each school, every quarter.[287] Social assistance for the children however is virtually non-existent upon release, and they invariably end up on the streets again, and often reoffending. All three boys we interviewed from borstals were on the streets and unemployed. Two were homeless.

Prisons

The Convention on the Rights of the Child requires that "every child deprived of liberty shall be separated from adults unless it is considered in the child's best interest not to do so."[288]

Under Kenyan law, children as young as fourteen years old may be sentenced to adult prisons by juvenile courts or transferred from approved schools and borstal institutions to adult prisons.[289] When a child is committed to adult prison the warrant of committal should clearly identify the child as a minor, and "where practicable" the child should be confined separately from adults and should not be allowed to associate with adult prisoners.[290]

Out of twenty-two children we interviewed who had been brought to court and were sentenced to deprivation of liberty, six were committed to adult prisons

---

[287] Human Rights Watch interview with Director of Probation and After-Care Services Joseph K. Gitau, Nairobi, September 16, 1996.

[288] Convention on the Rights of the Child, Article 37(c).

[289] Children and Young Persons Act, Article 46(b); Borstal Institutions Act, Article 42. A court order of committal is required for any such transfers.

[290] Children and Young Persons Act, Article 16. Under Rule 4 of the Prisons Rules, prisoners under the apparent age of seventeen are placed in the "young prisoner class."

for periods of between two weeks and two months. Five of those children were girls, who were all committed to Langata Prison for women in Nairobi. They were all convicted of "loitering with intent to solicit." All the girls were mixed with adult women in the prison. The girls said that prisoners are divided into different categories based on the length of their sentences. Girls who were confined in Langata in 1995 said that there were no mattresses and that they slept on the floor. Mattresses appear to have been added to the prison in 1996. "Things had changed the second time I was there. They had blankets, and mattresses, and they gave us Stay Free maxi pads. There were also new uniforms -- pink dresses," said fifteen-year-old Masi.[291] Girls said that punishments were beatings with a cane or a whip, made from an old rubber tire, usually for not doing their chores. They were made to work all day, digging in the *shamba*, carrying manure, mopping and cleaning, and hauling water. Serena described her imprisonment in Langata in 1996:

> They strip searched us when we arrived. We were naked and we had to jump up and down. We slept on small mattresses which were full of lice. We were given porridge in the morning at around 6 a.m., and then taken to the farm to work. We were closely supervised the whole time. At lunch, we were fed *ugali* and *sukuma wiki*, and then made to do more farm work. We had dinner at around 4 p.m. -- it was usually boiled potatoes. Then we'd go back to our room and sleep until they took roll call at 8 p.m. There were forty-four people in my room, girls and women all mixed together.[292]

The other child, a boy, was committed to Nairobi West Prison for one month. He was fourteen at the time, and had pled guilty to vagrancy.[293] He said he was the only boy there and that he was held with adults, who did not mistreat him. He and the other inmates slept on the floor, and he complained of hunger.

It is important to note that all six children were committed to prison by regular courts, not by juvenile court. It may be that the police and magistrate did not check the age of the children appearing before them, and believed them to be adults. As recommended earlier, police and magistrates should make diligent and

---

[291] Human Rights Watch interview with Masi, Nairobi, September 24, 1996.

[292] Human Rights Watch interview with Serena, Nairobi, September 24, 1996.

[293] Human Rights Watch interview with Paul, Nairobi, September 17, 1996..

systematic efforts to ascertain the true age of young people in their work, and ensure that children are properly identified and dealt with as children, not as adults.

VII. THE CHILDREN ACT

Following Kenya's ratification of the Convention on the Rights of the Child in 1990, the attorney general requested the Kenya Law Reform Commission to undertake a study of all laws relevant to children in Kenya, and to make recommendations for improvement and reform "so as to give effect to the spirit of the convention." The commission created the Child Law Task Force for this purpose. The Task Force began its study in August 1991 and issued its findings and recommendations in a comprehensive report in February 1993. Among other things, the Task Force recommended that a new law on children be enacted, to be referred to as the Children Act:

> The substance of the central statutes on child law, namely the Adoption Act, the Children and Young Person's Act, the Guardianship of Infants Act, and the Legitimacy Act, should be merged to form a new enactment which draws (as may be appropriate) on all statutes touching on children, incorporates relevant principles from the Convention on the Rights of the Child (1989), and attempts to resolve the various legal problems that affect the rights and welfare of children.[294]

Additionally, the Task Force recommended amendment of other existing statutes relevant to children and made other specific recommendations.

Following the recommendations of the Task Force, the government, through the Attorney General's Office, began the process of drafting the Children Bill (to become the Children's Act). The government sought the input of NGOs through occasional consultative meetings during the drafting of the bill. Little NGO input, however, was actually reflected in the resulting draft Children Bill. When the bill was presented to parliament in February 1995, it was met with widespread disappointment and criticism. Both KANU and opposition M.P.s, as well as local NGOs, faulted the bill for portraying child offenders as criminals in need of discipline and for failing to address homelessness and other problems afflicting children.[295] The attorney general withdrew the bill for redrafting. At the

---

[294] Report of the Child Law Task Force, on file with Human Rights Watch, Section 5.12, p. 121.

[295] U.S. Department of State, Kenya Country Report on Human Rights Practices for 1996, Section 5 (on Children).

time of the printing of this report, the redrafted bill has yet to be presented to parliament.

The bill was criticized for not addressing a wide range of children's issues, to which the attorney general responded that the bill is meant only to bring together three laws[296] identified by the Task Force; other laws and issues are to be dealt with separately, through legal reform and legal enactments, as well as policy and programmatic measures. "For example, there are such issues as child abuse, defilement, sexual exploitation, child prostitution and trafficking. This will be dealt with by making appropriate amendments to the Penal Code. . . If there is any issue affecting children which is covered under a particular legislation that issue will be dealt with under that particular legislation," the attorney general stated. He cautioned critics to remember that the bill should not be read in isolation of other efforts the government was undertaking to implement the Convention on the Rights of the Child.[297] Attorney General Wako further stated that the government is currently reviewing all legislation relevant to children and would publish proposed amendments soon. However, NGOs are wary of accepting such promises. "Yes, the penal code is supposed to be amended, as promised by the AG, but we've had a lot of promises," said Kimaru Wakaruru, Executive Director of the Child Welfare Society of Kenya and Chairman of the National Children in Need Network.[298] Human Rights Watch urges the government to make public its intentions and progress towards amending the other "at least sixteen different acts of Parliament [that] are to be amended," including the Penal Code and the Borstal Institutions Act.[299]

With regard to amendment of the three laws to be incorporated into the Children Act, the bill was criticized for being little more than the cutting and pasting together of the three existing statutes, with little substantive change. Indeed, with regard to the Children and Young Persons Act (the act which governs the juvenile court system in Kenya) the Children Bill appears to be virtually

---

[296] The Adoption Act, the Children and Young Persons Act, and the Guardianship of Infants Act.

[297] Speech by Attorney General Amos Wako, during the Official Opening of the Consultative Meeting on the Children's Bill, held at the Norfolk Hotel, Nairobi, May 17, 1996 ("Speech by Attorney General Wako"), on file with Human Rights Watch.

[298] Interview with Child Welfare Society.

[299] Speech by Attorney General Wako.

identical to existing law with a few significant changes. The distinctions in the Children and Young Persons Act between "child," "juvenile" and "young person" are eliminated; any person under the age of eighteen is to be referred to as a "child." Children under the age of eighteen are not to be confined with adults in police lockups, whereas under existing law only children under the age of sixteen are to be confined separately. A new category is established for children under ten years of age—"child of tender years." Juvenile courts are changed in name to "children's courts." However, in virtually all other respects, the language of the Children and Young Persons Act is unchanged. Children's courts can still commit children to "children's remand homes," remand prisons, approved schools, borstal institutions, and to regular prisons exactly as before—by the same procedures and on the same grounds (commission of criminal offenses and being "in need of protection or discipline.")

NGOS have repeatedly urged "that disciplinary matters be separated from protection matters pertaining to children in section 51 of the Children Bill," the section of the bill that defines children "in need of protection or discipline."[300] For example, Madeleine Njeri, program officer at the Kenya Alliance for the Advancement of Children, has been cited criticizing the continued combination of, and confusion between, discipline and protection matters; "the bill states that when a child is found begging [he or she] will be taken to a remand home, which means that that child is being disciplined and not being protected."[301] Thus the same problems that arose from the overlapping categorizations of "protection or discipline" and criminal matters under the Children and Young Persons Act are carried forward in the bill.

On a positive note, the bill contains prefatory language which places the "interests of the child" at the heart of any judicial decision-making affecting the child (Article 4):

> A court which or a person who exercises in respect of a child any powers conferred by this Act shall treat the interests of the child as the first and paramount consideration to the extent that this is consistent with adopting a course of action calculated to—

---

[300] A Statement from NGOs on the Children Bill, 1995, to the Consultative Meeting to be Held on 17th May, 1996 ("NGOs' Statement on 1995 Children Bill"), on file with Human Rights Watch, p. 3.

[301] Jemimah Mwakisha, "Nothing to Smile About," *The Nation* (Nairobi, Kenya), Wednesday Magazine, -- 1995.

> (a) secure for the child such guidance and correction as is necessary for the welfare of the child and in the public interest; and
>
> (b) conserve or promote, as far as possible, a satisfactory relationship between the child and other persons, whether within his family, his domestic environment or the community at large.

The bill also provides for the possibility of legal aid to children. Where a child is brought before a court and is unrepresented, the court may order that the child be granted legal representation, the cost of which shall be defrayed with funds provided by parliament to the minister of home affairs (Article 76). The bill also calls for the creation of a National Council of Children's Services consisting of nine high ranking government officials (including the police commissioner, and representatives from the President's Office and the Attorney General's Office) and nine NGO representatives (Article 22). The National Council would be responsible for formulating all government policies relating to child welfare. NGOs have urged that the council be authorized "to regulate, receive and act on all reports on children."[302]

Human Rights Watch recognizes the preliminary efforts of the Kenyan government to bring existing legislation into compliance with the Convention on the Rights of the Child, but urges the government to follow through with significant substantive change, lest the government's commitment to Kenyan children prove to be no more than lip service. The drafters of the Children Bill, under the Attorney General's Office, should consider fully the recommendations of NGOs, and NGO recommendations contained in the "Working Document: NGO Amendments to the Proposed Children Bill, 1995," in the ongoing drafting process. Further, specific recommendations on legislative reform are offered in Section 1 of this report.

---

[302] NGOs' Statement on 1995 Children Bill, p. 3.

VIII. CONCLUSION

The time is ripe for significant reform of the existing system of juvenile justice in Kenya. With the ongoing consideration of reform of the Children and Young Persons Act and a host of other laws effecting children, we hope that this report has provided some insights into the quandary that street children find themselves in their dealings with the juvenile justice system in Kenya, and the problems they face in the institutions where they are confined. While we recognize the urgent need for economic and social reforms to address the root causes of children taking to the streets, this report has focused on the need for reform of juvenile justice laws and practices, to combat violations of civil and political rights which street children continue to endure. The government made a stated commitment to reform existing laws to bring them into compliance with the Convention on the Rights of the Child. However, it has yet to be followed by the necessary action. The specific nature of the reforms, to be embodied in the long awaited Children Bill and other undetermined amendments and enactments, are yet to be seen. We strongly urge the government to consider the recommendations in this report and the input of local children's NGOs in the redrafting of the bill and in their other reform efforts. The redrafted Children Bill should be brought before parliament as soon as possible in order to enact the reformed legislation.

Particularly, we urge the government to ensure that the Children Bill clearly separates criminal from protection cases for children, and ensures that children receive all due process protections under international law when deprivation of liberty is at issue. We also urge the government to eliminate from existing laws and regulations all provisions authorizing corporal punishment, reduction in diet, and solitary confinement as punishment.

Finally, we recognize that legal reform is meaningless unless it is enforced. For this reason, we urge the government to ensure that those who work with children are specially educated and trained on how to handle cases of street children. Law enforcement personnel, the judiciary (and officers associated with juvenile court proceedings, children's officers and probation officers), and staff at correctional institutions should be sensitized to the special needs and rights of children with a view towards ensuring that the rights accorded to children, under international and Kenyan law, are respected and enforced. Related to this, all concerned governmental departments (including the Police Department, the Children's Department and the Prisons Department) should initiate prompt investigations into allegations of abuse of children by police and institutional staff, and to undertake disciplinary or criminal proceedings where appropriate, to ensure accountability of individual actors.

APPENDIX A:

Excerpts from the U.N. Convention on the Rights of the Child

U.N. Convention on the Rights of the Child, G.A. res. 44/25, annex, 44 U.N. GAOR Supp. (No. 49) at 167, U.N. Doc. A/44/49 (1989).

PREAMBLE

The States Parties to the present Convention,

Considering that, in accordance with the principles proclaimed in the Charter of the United Nations, recognition of the inherent dignity and of the equal and inalienable rights of all members of the human family is the foundation of freedom, justice and peace in the world,

Bearing in mind that the peoples of the United Nations have, in the Charter, reaffirmed their faith in fundamental human rights and in the dignity and worth of the human person, and have determined to promote social progress and better standards of life in larger freedom,

Recognizing that the United Nations has, in the Universal Declaration of Human Rights and in the International Covenants on Human Rights, proclaimed and agreed that everyone is entitled to all the rights and freedoms set forth therein, without distinction of any kind, such as race, colour, sex, language, religion, political or other opinion, national or social origin, property, birth or other status,

Recalling that, in the Universal Declaration of Human Rights, the United Nations has proclaimed that childhood is entitled to special care and assistance,

Convinced that the family, as the fundamental group of society and the natural environment for the growth and well-being of all its members and particularly children, should be afforded the necessary protection and assistance so that it can fully assume its responsibilities within the community,

Recognizing that the child, for the full and harmonious development of his or her personality, should grow up in a family environment, in an atmosphere of happiness, love and understanding,

Considering that the child should be fully prepared to live an individual life in society, and brought up in the spirit of the ideals proclaimed in the Charter of the United Nations, and in particular in the spirit of peace, dignity, tolerance, freedom, equality and solidarity,

Bearing in mind that the need to extend particular care to the child has been stated in the Geneva Declaration of the Rights of the Child of 1924 and in the Declaration of the Rights of the Child adopted by the General Assembly on 20 November 1959 and recognized in the Universal Declaration of Human Rights, in the International Covenant on Civil and Political Rights (in particular in articles 23 and 24), in the International Covenant on Economic, Social and Cultural Rights (in particular in article 10) and in the statutes and relevant instruments of specialized agencies and international organizations concerned with the welfare of children, '

Bearing in mind that, as indicated in the Declaration of the Rights of the Child, "the child, by reason of his physical and mental immaturity, needs special safeguards and care, including appropriate legal protection, before as well as after birth,"

Recalling the provisions of the Declaration on Social and Legal Principles relating to the Protection and Welfare of Children, with Special Reference to Foster Placement and Adoption Nationally and Internationally; the United Nations Standard Minimum Rules for the Administration of Juvenile Justice (The Beijing Rules) ; and the Declaration on the Protection of Women and Children in Emergency and Armed Conflict,

Recognizing that, in all countries in the world, there are children living in exceptionally difficult conditions, and that such children need special consideration,

Taking due account of the importance of the traditions and cultural values of each people for the protection and harmonious development of the child,

Recognizing the importance of international co-operation for improving the living conditions of children in every country, in particular in the developing countries,

Have agreed as follows:

PART I

Article 1

For the purposes of the present Convention, a child means every human being below the age of eighteen years unless under the law applicable to the child, majority is attained earlier.

Article 3

1. In all actions concerning children, whether undertaken by public or private social welfare institutions, courts of law, administrative authorities or legislative bodies, the best interests of the child shall be a primary consideration.
2. States Parties undertake to ensure the child such protection and care as is necessary for his or her well-being, taking into account the rights and duties of his or her parents, legal guardians, or other individuals legally responsible for him or her, and, to this end, shall take all appropriate legislative and administrative measures.
3. States Parties shall ensure that the institutions, services and facilities responsible for the care or protection of children shall conform with the standards established by competent authorities, particularly in the areas of safety, health, in the number and suitability of their staff, as well as competent supervision.

Article 4

States Parties shall undertake all appropriate legislative, administrative, and other measures for the implementation of the rights recognized in the present Convention. With regard to economic, social and cultural rights, States Parties shall undertake such measures to the maximum extent of their available resources and, where needed, within the framework of international co-operation.

Article 5

States Parties shall respect the responsibilities, rights and duties of parents or, where applicable, the members of the extended family or community as provided for by local custom, legal guardians or other persons legally responsible for the child, to provide, in a manner consistent with the evolving capacities of the child, appropriate direction and guidance in the exercise by the child of the rights recognized in the present Convention.

Article 6

1. States Parties recognize that every child has the inherent right to life.

2. States Parties shall ensure to the maximum extent possible the survival and development of the child.

Article 9

1. States Parties shall ensure that a child shall not be separated from his or her parents against their will, except when competent authorities subject to judicial review determine, in accordance with applicable law and procedures, that such separation is necessary for the best interests of the child. Such determination may be necessary in a particular case such as one involving abuse or neglect of the child by the parents, or one where the parents are living separately and a decision must be made as to the child's place of residence.
2. In any proceedings pursuant to paragraph 1 of the present article, all interested parties shall be given an opportunity to participate in the proceedings and make their views known.
3. States Parties shall respect the right of the child who is separated from one or both parents to maintain personal relations and direct contact with both parents on a regular basis, except if it is contrary to the child's best interests.
4. Where such separation results from any action initiated by a State Party, such as the detention, imprisonment, exile, deportation or death (including death arising from any cause while the person is in the custody of the State) of one or both parents or of the child, that State Party shall, upon request, provide the parents, the child or, if appropriate, another member of the family with the essential information concerning the whereabouts of the absent member(s) of the family unless the provision of the information would be detrimental to the well-being of the child. States Parties shall further ensure that the submission of such a request shall of itself entail no adverse consequences for the person(s) concerned.

Article 15

1. States Parties recognize the rights of the child to freedom of association and to freedom of peaceful assembly.
2. No restrictions may be placed on the exercise of these rights other than those imposed in conformity with the law and which are necessary in a democratic society in the interests of national security or public safety, public order (ordre public), the protection of public health or morals or the protection of the rights and freedoms of others.

Article 16

1. No child shall be subjected to arbitrary or unlawful interference with his or her privacy, family, home or correspondence, nor to unlawful attacks on his or her honour and reputation.
2. The child has the right to the protection of the law against such interference or attacks.

Article 18

1. States Parties shall use their best efforts to ensure recognition of the principle that both parents have common responsibilities for the upbringing and development of the child. Parents or, as the case may be, legal guardians, have the primary responsibility for the upbringing and development of the child. The best interests of the child will be their basic concern.
2. For the purpose of guaranteeing and promoting the rights set forth in the present Convention, States Parties shall render appropriate assistance to parents and legal guardians in the performance of their child-rearing responsibilities and shall ensure the development of institutions, facilities and services for the care of children.
3. States Parties shall take all appropriate measures to ensure that children of working parents have the right to benefit from child-care services and facilities for which they are eligible.

Article 19

1. States Parties shall take all appropriate legislative, administrative, social and educational measures to protect the child from all forms of physical or mental violence, injury or abuse, neglect or negligent treatment, maltreatment or exploitation, including sexual abuse, while in the care of parent(s), legal guardian(s) or any other person who has the care of the child.
2. Such protective measures should, as appropriate, include effective procedures for the establishment of social programmes to provide necessary support for the child and for those who have the care of the child, as well as for other forms of prevention and for identification, reporting, referral, investigation, treatment and follow-up of instances of child maltreatment described heretofore, and, as appropriate, for judicial involvement.

Article 20

1. A child temporarily or permanently deprived of his or her family environment, or in whose own best interests cannot be allowed to remain in that environment, shall be entitled to special protection and assistance provided by the State.

2. States Parties shall in accordance with their national laws ensure alternative care for such a child.
3. Such care could include, inter alia, foster placement, kafalah of Islamic law, adoption or if necessary placement in suitable institutions for the care of children. When considering solutions, due regard shall be paid to the desirability of continuity in a child's upbringing and to the child's ethnic, religious, cultural and linguistic background.

Article 25

States Parties recognize the right of a child who has been placed by the competent authorities for the purposes of care, protection or treatment of his or her physical or mental health, to a periodic review of the treatment provided to the child and all other circumstances relevant to his or her placement.

Article 28

1. States Parties recognize the right of the child to education, and with a view to achieving this right progressively and on the basis of equal opportunity, they shall, in particular:
(a) Make primary education compulsory and available free to all;
(b) Encourage the development of different forms of secondary education, including general and vocational education, make them available and accessible to every child, and take appropriate measures such as the introduction of free education and offering financial assistance in case of need;
(c) Make higher education accessible to all on the basis of capacity by every appropriate means;
(d) Make educational and vocational information and guidance available and accessible to all children;
(e) Take measures to encourage regular attendance at schools and the reduction of drop-out rates.
2. States Parties shall take all appropriate measures to ensure that school discipline is administered in a manner consistent with the child's human dignity and in conformity with the present Convention.
3. States Parties shall promote and encourage international cooperation in matters relating to education, in particular with a view to contributing to the elimination of ignorance and illiteracy throughout the world and facilitating access to scientific and technical knowledge and modern teaching methods. In this regard, particular account shall be taken of the needs of developing countries.

Article 29

1. States Parties agree that the education of the child shall be directed to:

(a) The development of the child's personality, talents and mental and physical abilities to their fullest potential;

(b) The development of respect for human rights and fundamental freedoms, and for the principles enshrined in the Charter of the United Nations;

(c)The development of respect for the child's parents, his or her own cultural identity, language and values, for the national values of the country in which the child is living, the country from which he or she may originate, and for civilizations different from his or her own;

(d) The preparation of the child for responsible life in a free society, in the spirit of understanding, peace, tolerance, equality of sexes, and friendship among all peoples, ethnic, national and religious groups and persons of indigenous origin;

(e) The development of respect for the natural environment.

2. No part of the present article or article 28 shall be construed so as to interfere with the liberty of individuals and bodies to establish and direct educational institutions, subject always to the observance of the principle set forth in paragraph 1 of the present article and to the requirements that the education given in such institutions shall conform to such minimum standards as may be laid down by the State.

Article 34

States Parties undertake to protect the child from all forms of sexual exploitation and sexual abuse. For these purposes, States Parties shall in particular take all appropriate national, bilateral and multilateral measures to prevent:

(a) The inducement or coercion of a child to engage in any unlawful sexual activity;

(b) The exploitative use of children in prostitution or other unlawful sexual practices;

(c) The exploitative use of children in pornographic performances and materials.

Article 36

States Parties shall protect the child against all other forms of exploitation prejudicial to any aspects of the child's welfare.

Article 37

States Parties shall ensure that:

(a) No child shall be subjected to torture or other cruel, inhuman or degrading treatment or punishment. Neither capital punishment nor life imprisonment without possibility of release shall be imposed for offenses committed by persons below eighteen years of age;

(b) No child shall be deprived of his or her liberty unlawfully or arbitrarily. The arrest, detention or imprisonment of a child shall be in conformity with the law and shall be used only as a measure of last resort and for the shortest appropriate period of time;

(c) Every child deprived of liberty shall be treated with humanity and respect for the inherent dignity of the human person, and in a manner which takes into account the needs of persons of his or her age. In particular, every child deprived of liberty shall be separated from adults unless it is considered in the child's best interest not to do so and shall have the right to maintain contact with his or her family through correspondence and visits, save in exceptional circumstances;

(d) Every child deprived of his or her liberty shall have the right to prompt access to legal and other appropriate assistance, as well as the right to challenge the legality of the deprivation of his or her liberty before a court or other competent, independent and impartial authority, and to a prompt decision on any such action.

Article 40

1. States Parties recognize the right of every child alleged as, accused of, or recognized as having infringed the penal law to be treated in a manner consistent with the promotion of the child's sense of dignity and worth, which reinforces the child's respect for the human rights and fundamental freedoms of others and which takes into account the child's age and the desirability of promoting the child's reintegration and the child's assuming a constructive role in society.

2. To this end, and having regard to the relevant provisions of international instruments, States Parties shall, in particular, ensure that:

(a) No child shall be alleged as, be accused of, or recognized as having infringed the penal law by reason of acts or omissions that were not prohibited by national or international law at the time they were committed;

(b) Every child alleged as or accused of having infringed the penal law has at least the following guarantees:

>(i) To be presumed innocent until proven guilty according to law;
>
>(ii) To be informed promptly and directly of the charges against him or her, and, if appropriate, through his or her parents or legal guardians, and to have legal or other appropriate assistance in the preparation and presentation of his or her defense;
>
>(iii) To have the matter determined without delay by a competent, independent and impartial authority or judicial body

in a fair hearing according to law, in the presence of legal or other appropriate assistance and, unless it is considered not to be in the best interest of the child, in particular, taking into account his or her age or situation, his or her parents or legal guardians;

(iv) Not to be compelled to give testimony or to confess guilt; to examine or have examined adverse witnesses and to obtain the participation and examination of witnesses on his or her behalf under conditions of equality;

(v) If considered to have infringed the penal law, to have this decision and any measures imposed in consequence thereof reviewed by a higher competent, independent and impartial authority or judicial body according to law;

(vi) To have the free assistance of an interpreter if the child cannot understand or speak the language used;

(vii) To have his or her privacy fully respected at all stages of the proceedings. 3. States Parties shall seek to promote the establishment of laws, procedures, authorities and institutions specifically applicable to children alleged as, accused of, or recognized as having infringed the penal law, and, in particular:

3. States Parties shall seek to promote the establishment of laws, procedures, authorities and institutions specifically applicable to children alleged as, accused of, or recognized as having infringed the penal law, in particular:

(a) The establishment of a minimum age below which children shall be presumed not to have the capacity to infringe the penal law;

(b) Whenever appropriate and desirable, measures for dealing with such children without resorting to judicial proceedings, providing that human rights and legal safeguards are fully respected.

4. A variety of dispositions, such as care, guidance and supervision orders; counseling; probation; foster care; education and vocational training programmes and other alternatives to institutional care shall be available to ensure that children are dealt with in a manner appropriate to their well-being and proportionate both to their circumstances and the offense.

Article 41

Nothing in the present Convention shall affect any provisions which are more conducive to the realization of the rights of the child and which may be contained in:

(a) The law of a State party; or
(b) International law in force for that State.

APPENDIX B:

U.N. Standard Minimum Rules For The Administration of Juvenile Justice

United Nations Standard Minimum Rules for the Administration of Juvenile Justice ("The Beijing Rules"), G.A. res. 40/33, annex, 40 U.N. GAOR Supp. (No. 53) at 207, U.N. Doc. A/40/53 (1985).

PART ONE

General principles

1. Fundamental perspectives
1.1 Member States shall seek, in conformity with their respective general interests, to further the well-being of the juvenile and her or his family.
1.2 Member States shall endeavor to develop conditions that will ensure for the juvenile a meaningful life in the community, which, during that period in life when she or he is most susceptible to deviant behavior, will foster a process of personal development and education that is as free from crime and delinquency as possible.
1.3 Sufficient attention shall be given to positive measures that involve the full mobilization of all possible resources, including the family, volunteers and other community groups, as well as schools and other community institutions, for the purpose of promoting the well-being of the juvenile, with a view to reducing the need for intervention under the law, and of effectively, fairly and humanely dealing with the juvenile in conflict with the law.
1.4 Juvenile justice shall be conceived as an integral part of the national development process of each country, within a comprehensive framework of social justice for all juveniles, thus, at the same time, contributing to the protection of the young and the maintenance of a peaceful order in society.
1.5 These Rules shall be implemented in the context of economic, social and cultural conditions prevailing in each Member State.
1.6 Juvenile justice services shall be systematically developed and coordinated with a view to improving and sustaining the competence of personnel involved in the services, including their methods, approaches and attitudes.

2. Scope of the Rules and definitions used
2.1 The following Standard Minimum Rules shall be applied to juvenile offenders impartially, without distinction of any kind, for example as to race, color, sex,

language, religion, political or other opinions, national or social origin, property, birth or other status.

2.2 For purposes of these Rules, the following definitions shall be applied by Member States in a manner which is compatible with their respective legal systems and concepts:

>(a) A juvenile is a child or young person who, under the respective legal systems, may be dealt with for an offense in a manner which is different from an adult;
>
>(b) An offense is any behavior (act or omission) that is punishable by law under the respective legal system;
>
>(c) A juvenile offender is a child or young person who is alleged to have committed or who has been found to have committed an offense.

2.3 Efforts shall be made to establish, in each national jurisdiction, a set of laws, rules and provisions specifically applicable to juvenile offenders and institutions and bodies entrusted with the functions of the administration of juvenile justice and designed:

>(a) To meet the varying needs of juvenile offenders, while protecting their basic rights;
>
>(b) To meet the needs of society;
>
>(c) To implement the following rules thoroughly and fairly.

3. Extension of the Rules

3.1 The relevant provisions of the Rules shall be applied not only to juvenile offenders but also to juveniles who may be proceeded against for any specific behavior that would not be punishable if committed by an adult.

3.2 Efforts shall be made to extend the principles embodied in the Rules to all juveniles who are dealt with in welfare and care proceedings.

3.3 Efforts shall also be made to extend the principles embodied in the Rules to young adult offenders.

4. Age of criminal responsibility

4.1 In those legal systems recognizing the concept of the age of criminal responsibility for juveniles, the beginning of that age shall not be fixed at too low an age level, bearing in mind the facts of emotional, mental and intellectual maturity.

5. Aims of juvenile justice
5. 1 The juvenile justice system shall emphasize the well-being of the juvenile and shall ensure that any reaction to juvenile offenders shall always be in proportion to the circumstances of both the offenders and the offense.

6. Scope of discretion
6.1 In view of the varying special needs of juveniles as well as the variety of measures available, appropriate scope for discretion shall be allowed at all stages of proceedings and at the different levels of juvenile justice administration, including investigation, prosecution, adjudication and the follow-up of dispositions.
6.2 Efforts shall be made, however, to ensure sufficient accountability at all stages and levels in the exercise of any such discretion.
6.3 Those who exercise discretion shall be specially qualified or trained to exercise it judiciously and in accordance with their functions and mandates.

7. Rights of juveniles
7.1 Basic procedural safeguards such as the presumption of innocence, the right to be notified of the charges, the right to remain silent, the right to counsel, the right to the presence of a parent or guardian, the right to confront and cross-examine witnesses and the right to appeal to a higher authority shall be guaranteed at all stages of proceedings.

8. Protection of privacy
8.1 The juvenile's right to privacy shall be respected at all stages in order to avoid harm being caused to her or him by undue publicity or by the process of labeling.
8.2 In principle, no information that may lead to the identification of a juvenile offender shall be published.

9. Saving clause
9.1 Nothing in these Rules shall be interpreted as precluding the application of the Standard Minimum Rules for the Treatment of Prisoners adopted by the United Nations and other human rights instruments and standards recognized by the international community that relate to the care and protection of the young.

PART TWO

Investigation and prosecution

10. Initial contact
10.1 Upon the apprehension of a juvenile, her or his parents or guardian shall be immediately notified of such apprehension, and, where such immediate notification is not possible, the parents or guardian shall be notified within the shortest possible time thereafter.
10.2 A judge or other competent official or body shall, without delay, consider the issue of release.
10.3 Contacts between the law enforcement agencies and a juvenile offender shall be managed in such a way as to respect the legal status of the juvenile, promote the well-being of the juvenile and avoid harm to her or hi m, with due regard to the circumstances of the case.

11. Diversion
11.1 Consideration shall be given, wherever appropriate, to dealing with juvenile offenders without resorting to formal trial by the competent authority, referred to in rule 14.1 below.
11.2 The police, the prosecution or other agencies dealing with juvenile cases shall be empowered to dispose of such cases, at their discretion, without recourse to formal hearings, in accordance with the criteria laid down for that purpose in the respective legal system and also in accordance with the principles contained in these Rules.
11.3 Any diversion involving referral to appropriate community or other services shall require the consent of the juvenile, or her or his parents or guardian, provided that such decision to refer a case shall be subject to review by a competent authority, upon application.
11.4 In order to facilitate the discretionary disposition of juvenile cases, efforts shall be made to provide for community programmes, such as temporary supervision and guidance, restitution, and compensation of victims.

12. Specialization within the police
12.1 In order to best fulfil their functions, police officers who frequently or exclusively deal with juveniles or who are primarily engaged in the prevention of juvenile crime shall be specially instructed and trained. In large cities, special police units should be established for that purpose.

13. Detention pending trial

13.1 Detention pending trial shall be used only as a measure of last resort and for the shortest possible period of time.

13.2 Whenever possible, detention pending trial shall be replaced by alternative measures, such as close supervision, intensive care or placement with a family or in an educational setting or home.

13.3 Juveniles under detention pending trial shall be entitled to all rights and guarantees of the Standard Minimum Rules for the Treatment of Prisoners adopted by the United Nations.

13.4 Juveniles under detention pending trial shall be kept separate from adults and shall be detained in a separate institution or in a separate part of an institution also holding adults.

13.5 While in custody, juveniles shall receive care, protection and all necessary individual assistance-social, educational, vocational, psychological, medical and physical-that they may require in view of their age, sex and personality.

PART THREE

Adjudication and disposition

14. Competent authority to adjudicate

14.1 Where the case of a juvenile offender has not been diverted (under rule 11), she or he shall be dealt with by the competent authority (court, tribunal, board, council, etc.) according to the principles of a fair and just trial.

14.2 The proceedings shall be conducive to the best interests of the juvenile and shall be conducted in an atmosphere of understanding, which shall allow the juvenile to participate therein and to express herself or himself freely.

15. Legal counsel, parents and guardians

15.1 Throughout the proceedings the juvenile shall have the right to be represented by a legal adviser or to apply for free legal aid where there is provision for such aid in the country.

15.2 The parents or the guardian shall be entitled to participate in the proceedings and may be required by the competent authority to attend them in the interest of the juvenile. They may, however, be denied participation by the competent authority if there are reasons to assume that such exclusion is necessary in the interest of the juvenile.

16. Social inquiry reports

16.1 In all cases except those involving minor offenses, before the competent authority renders a final disposition prior to sentencing, the background and circumstances in which the juvenile is living or the conditions under which the offense has been committed shall be properly investigated so as to facilitate judicious adjudication of the case by the competent authority.

17. Guiding principles in adjudication and disposition

17.1 The disposition of the competent authority shall be guided by the following principles:

(a) The reaction taken shall always be in proportion not only to the circumstances and the gravity of the offense but also to the circumstances and the needs of the juvenile as well as to the needs of the society;

(b) Restrictions on the personal liberty of the juvenile shall be imposed only after careful consideration and shall be limited to the possible minimum;

(c) Deprivation of personal liberty shall not be imposed unless the juvenile is adjudicated of a serious act involving violence against another person or of persistence in committing other serious offenses and unless there is no other appropriate response;

(d) The well-being of the juvenile shall be the guiding factor in the consideration of her or his case.

17.2 Capital punishment shall not be imposed for any crime committed by juveniles.

17.3 Juveniles shall not be subject to corporal punishment.

17.4 The competent authority shall have the power to discontinue the proceedings at any time.

18. Various disposition measures

18.1 A large variety of disposition measures shall be made available to the competent authority, allowing for flexibility so as to avoid institutionalization to the greatest extent possible. Such measures, some of which may be combined, include:

(a) Care, guidance and supervision orders;
(b) Probation;
(c) Community service orders;
(d) Financial penalties, compensation and restitution;

(e) Intermediate treatment and other treatment orders;
(f) Orders to participate in group counseling and similar activities;
(g) Orders concerning foster care, living communities or other educational settings;
(h) Other relevant orders.

18.2 No juvenile shall be removed from parental supervision, whether partly or entire l y, unless the circumstances of her or his case make this necessary.

19. Least possible use of institutionalization

19.1 The placement of a juvenile in an institution shall always be a disposition of last resort and for the minimum necessary period.

20. Avoidance of unnecessary delay

20.1 Each case shall from the outset be handled expeditiously, without any unnecessary delay.

21. Records

21.1 Records of juvenile offenders shall be kept strictly confidential and closed to third parties. Access to such records shall be limited to persons directly concerned with the disposition of the case at hand or other duly authorized persons.

21.2 Records of juvenile offenders shall not be used in adult proceedings in subsequent cases involving the same offender.

22. Need for professionalism and training

22.1 Professional education, in-service training, refresher courses and other appropriate modes of instruction shall be utilized to establish and maintain the necessary professional competence of all personnel dealing with juvenile cases.

22.2 Juvenile justice personnel shall reflect the diversity of juveniles who come into contact with the juvenile justice system. Efforts shall be made to ensure the fair representation of women and minorities in juvenile justice agencies.

PART FOUR

Non-institutional treatment

23. Effective implementation of disposition
23.1 Appropriate provisions shall be made for the implementation of orders of the competent authority, as referred to in rule 14.1 above, by that authority itself or by some other authority as circumstances may require.
23.2 Such provisions shall include the power to modify the orders as the competent authority may deem necessary from time to time, provided that such modification shall be determined in accordance with the principles contained in these Rules.

24. Provision of needed assistance
24.1 Efforts shall be made to provide juveniles, at all stages of the proceedings, with necessary assistance such as lodging, education or vocational training, employment or any other assistance, helpful and practical, in order to facilitate the rehabilitative process.

25. Mobilization of volunteers and other community services
25.1 Volunteers, voluntary organizations, local institutions and other community resources shall be called upon to contribute effectively to the rehabilitation of the juvenile in a community setting and, as far as possible, within the family unit.

PART FIVE

Institutional treatment

26. Objectives of institutional treatment
26.1 The objective of training and treatment of juveniles placed in institutions is to provide care, protection, education and vocational skills, with a view to assisting them to assume socially constructive and productive roles in society.
26.2 Juveniles in institutions shall receive care, protection and all necessary assistance-social, educational, vocational, psychological, medical and physical-that they may require because of their age, sex, and personality and in the interest of their wholesome development .

26.3 Juveniles in institutions shall be kept separate from adults and shall be detained in a separate institution or in a separate part of an institution also holding adults.

26.4 Young female offenders placed in an institution deserve special attention as to their personal needs and problems. They shall by no means receive less care, protection, assistance, treatment and training than young male offenders. Their fair treatment shall be ensured.

26.5 In the interest and well-being of the institutionalized juvenile, the parents or guardians shall have a right of access.

26.6 Inter-ministerial and inter-departmental co-operation shall be fostered for the purpose of providing adequate academic or, as appropriate, vocational training to institutionalized juveniles, with a view to ensuring that they do no leave the institution at an educational disadvantage.

27. *Application of the Standard Minimum Rules for the Treatment of Prisoners adopted by the United Nations*

27.1 The Standard Minimum Rules for the Treatment of Prisoners and related recommendations shall be applicable as far as relevant to the treatment of juvenile offenders in institutions, including those in detention pending adjudication.

27.2 Efforts shall be made to implement the relevant principles laid down in the Standard Minimum Rules for the Treatment of Prisoners to the largest possible extent so as to meet the varying needs of juveniles specific to their age, sex and personality.

28. *Frequent and early recourse to conditional release*

28.1 Conditional release from an institution shall be used by the appropriate authority to the greatest possible extent, and shall be granted at the earliest possible time.

28.2 Juveniles released conditionally from an institution shall be assisted and supervised by an appropriate authority and shall receive full support by the community.

29. *Semi-institutional arrangements*

29.1 Efforts shall be made to provide semi-institutional arrangements, such as half-way houses, educational homes, day-time training centers and other such appropriate arrangements that may assist juveniles in their proper reintegration into society.

PART SIX

Research, planning, policy formulation and evaluation

30. Research as a basis for planning, policy formulation and evaluation
30.1 Efforts shall be made to organize and promote necessary research as a basis for effective planning and policy formulation.
30.2 Efforts shall be made to review and appraise periodically the trends, problems and causes of juvenile delinquency and crime as well as the varying particular needs of juveniles in custody.
30.3 Efforts shall be made to establish a regular evaluative research mechanism built into the system of juvenile justice administration and to collect and analyze relevant data and information for appropriate assessment and future improvement and reform of the administration.
30.4 The delivery of services in juvenile justice administration shall be systematically planned and implemented as an integral part of national development efforts.

APPENDIX C:

U.N. Rules For The Protection of Juveniles Deprived of Their Liberty

U.N. Rules for the Protection of Juveniles Deprived of their Liberty, G.A. res. 45/113, annex, 45 U.N. GAOR Supp. (No. 49A) at 205, U.N. Doc. A/45/49 (1990).

I. Fundamental perspectives

1. The juvenile justice system should uphold the rights and safety and promote the physical and mental well-being of juveniles. Imprisonment should be used as a last resort.
2. Juveniles should only be deprived of their liberty in accordance with the principles and procedures set forth in these Rules and in the United Nations Standard Minimum Rules for the Administration of Juvenile Justice (The Beijing Rules). Deprivation of the liberty of a juvenile should be a disposition of last resort and for the minimum necessary period and should be limited to exceptional cases. The length of the sanction should be determined by the judicial authority, without precluding the possibility of his or her early release.
3. The Rules are intended to establish minimum standards accepted by the United Nations for the protection of juveniles deprived of their liberty in all forms, consistent with human rights and fundamental freedoms, and with a view to counteracting the detrimental effects of all types of detention and to fostering integration in society.
4. The Rules should be applied impartially, without discrimination of any kind as to race, color, sex, age, language, religion, nationality, political or other opinion, cultural beliefs or practices, property, birth or family status, ethnic or social origin, and disability. The religious and cultural beliefs, practices and moral concepts of the juvenile should be respected.
5. The Rules are designed to serve as convenient standards of reference and to provide encouragement and guidance to professionals involved in the management of the juvenile justice system.
6. The Rules should be made readily available to juvenile justice personnel in their national languages. Juveniles who are not fluent in the language spoken by the personnel of the detention facility should have the right to the services of an

interpreter free of charge whenever necessary, in particular during medical examinations and disciplinary proceedings.

7. Where appropriate, States should incorporate the Rules into their legislation or amend it accordingly and provide effective remedies for their breach, including compensation when injuries are inflicted on juveniles. States should also monitor the application of the Rules.

8. The competent authorities should constantly seek to increase the awareness of the public that the care of detained juveniles and preparation for their return to society is a social service of great importance, and to this end active steps should be taken to foster open contacts between the juveniles and the local community.

9. Nothing in the Rules should be interpreted as precluding the application of the relevant United Nations and human rights instruments and standards, recognized by the international community, that are more conducive to ensuring the rights, care and protection of juveniles, children and all young persons.

10. In the event that the practical application of particular Rules contained in sections II to V, inclusive, presents any conflict with the Rules contained in the present section, compliance with the latter shall be regarded as the predominant requirement.

II. Scope and application of the rules

11. For the purposes of the Rules, the following definitions should apply:
    (a) A juvenile is every person under the age of 18. The age limit below which it should not be permitted to deprive a child of his or her liberty should be determined by law;
    (b) The deprivation of liberty means any form of detention or imprisonment or the placement of a person in a public or private custodial setting, from which this person is not permitted to leave at will, by order of any judicial, administrative or other public authority.

12. The deprivation of liberty should be effected in conditions and circumstances which ensure respect for the human rights of juveniles. Juveniles detained in facilities should be guaranteed the benefit of meaningful activities and programmes which would serve to promote and sustain their health and self-respect, to foster their sense of responsibility and encourage those attitudes and skills that will assist them in developing their potential as members of society.

13. Juveniles deprived of their liberty shall not for any reason related to their status be denied the civil, economic, political, social or cultural rights to which they are

entitled under national or international law, and which are compatible with the deprivation of liberty.

14. The protection of the individual rights of juveniles with special regard to the legality of the execution of the detention measures shall be ensured by the competent authority, while the objectives of social integration should be secured by regular inspections and other means of control carried out, according to international standards, national laws and regulations, by a duly constituted body authorized to visit the juveniles and not belonging to the detention facility.

15. The Rules apply to all types and forms of detention facilities in which juveniles are deprived of their liberty. Sections I, II, IV and V of the Rules apply to all detention facilities and institutional settings in which juveniles are detained, and section III applies specifically to juveniles under arrest or awaiting trial.

16. The Rules shall be implemented in the context of the economic, social and cultural conditions prevailing in each Member State.

III. Juveniles under arrest or awaiting trial

17. Juveniles who are detained under arrest or awaiting trial ("untried") are presumed innocent and shall be treated as such. Detention before trial shall be avoided to the extent possible and limited to exceptional circumstances. Therefore, all efforts shall be made to apply alternative measures. When preventive detention is nevertheless used, juvenile courts and investigative bodies shall give the highest priority to the most expeditious processing of such cases to ensure the shortest possible duration of detention. Untried detainees should be separated from convicted juveniles.

18. The conditions under which an untried juvenile is detained should be consistent with the rules set out below, with additional specific provisions as are necessary and appropriate, given the requirements of the presumption of innocence, the duration of the detention and the legal status and circumstances of the juvenile. These provisions would include, but not necessarily be restricted to, the following:

(a) Juveniles should have the right of legal counsel and be enabled to apply for free legal aid, where such aid is available, and to communicate regularly with their legal advisers. Privacy and confidentiality shall be ensured for such communications;

(b) Juveniles should be provided, where possible, with opportunities to pursue work, with remuneration, and continue education or training, but should not be required to do so. Work, education or training should not cause the continuation of the detention;

(c) Juveniles should receive and retain materials for their leisure and recreation as are compatible with the interests of the administration of justice.

IV. The management of juvenile facilities

A. Records

19. All reports, including legal records, medical records and records of disciplinary proceedings, and all other documents relating to the form, content and details of treatment, should be placed in a confidential individual file, which should be kept up to date, accessible only to authorized persons and classified in such a way as to be easily understood. Where possible, every juvenile should have the right to contest any fact or opinion contained in his or her file so as to permit rectification of inaccurate, unfounded or unfair statements. In order to exercise this right, there should be procedures that allow an appropriate third party to have access to and to consult the file on request. Upon release, the records of juveniles shall be sealed, and, at an appropriate time, expunged.

20. No juvenile should be received in any detention facility without a valid commitment order of a judicial, administrative or other public authority. The details of this order should be immediately entered in the register. No juvenile should be detained in any facility where there is no such register.

B. Admission, registration, movement and transfer

21. In every place where juveniles are detained, a complete and secure record of the following information should be kept concerning each juvenile received:
> (a) Information on the identity of the juvenile;
> (b) The fact of and reasons for commitment and the authority therefor;
> (c) The day and hour of admission, transfer and release;
> (d) Details of the notifications to parents and guardians on every admission, transfer or release of the juvenile in their care at the time of commitment;
> (e) Details of known physical and mental health problems, including drug and alcohol abuse.

22. The information on admission, place, transfer and release should be provided without delay to the parents and guardians or closest relative of the juvenile concerned.

23. As soon as possible after reception, full reports and relevant information on the personal situation and circumstances of each juvenile should be drawn up and submitted to the administration.

24. On admission, all juveniles shall be given a copy of the rules governing the detention facility and a written description of their rights and obligations in a language they can understand, together with the address of the authorities competent to receive complaints, as well as the address of public or private agencies and organizations which provide legal assistance. For those juveniles who are illiterate or who cannot understand the language in the written form, the information should be conveyed in a manner enabling full comprehension.

25. All juveniles should be helped to understand the regulations governing the internal organization of the facility, the goals and methodology of the care provided, the disciplinary requirements and procedures, other authorized methods of seeking information and of making complaints and all such other matters as are necessary to enable them to understand fully their rights and obligations during detention.

26. The transport of juveniles should be carried out at the expense of the administration in conveyances with adequate ventilation and light, in conditions that should in no way subject them to hardship or indignity. Juveniles should not be transferred from one facility to another arbitrarily.

C. *Classification and placement*

27. As soon as possible after the moment of admission, each juvenile should be interviewed, and a psychological and social report identifying any factors relevant to the specific type and level of care and programme required by the juvenile should be prepared. This report, together with the report prepared by a medical officer who has examined the juvenile upon admission, should be forwarded to the director for purposes of determining the most appropriate placement for the juvenile within the facility and the specific type and level of care and programme required and to be pursued. When special rehabilitative treatment is required, and the length of stay in the facility permits, trained personnel of the facility should prepare a written, individualized treatment plan specifying treatment objectives and time-frame and the means, stages and delays with which the objectives should be approached.

28. The detention of juveniles should only take place under conditions that take full account of their particular needs, status and special requirements according to their age, personality, sex and type of offense, as well as mental and physical health, and which ensure their protection from harmful influences and risk situations. The principal criterion for the separation of different categories of

juveniles deprived of their liberty should be the provision of the type of care best suited to the particular needs of the individuals concerned and the protection of their physical, mental and moral integrity and well-being.

29. In all detention facilities juveniles should be separated from adults, unless they are members of the same family. Under controlled conditions, juveniles may be brought together with carefully selected adults as part of a special programme that has been shown to be beneficial for the juveniles concerned.

30. Open detention facilities for juveniles should be established. Open detention facilities are those with no or minimal security measures. The population in such detention facilities should be as small as possible. The number of juveniles detained in closed facilities should be small enough to enable individualized treatment. Detention facilities for juveniles should be decentralized and of such size as to facilitate access and contact between the juveniles and their families. Small-scale detention facilities should be established and integrated into the social, economic and cultural environment of the community.

D. *Physical environment and accommodation*

31. Juveniles deprived of their liberty have the right to facilities and services that meet all the requirements of health and human dignity.

32. The design of detention facilities for juveniles and the physical environment should be in keeping with the rehabilitative aim of residential treatment, with due regard to the need of the juvenile for privacy, sensory stimuli, opportunities for association with peers and participation in sports, physical exercise and leisure-time activities. The design and structure of juvenile detention facilities should be such as to minimize the risk of fire and to ensure safe evacuation from the premises. There should be an effective alarm system in case of fire, as well as formal and drilled procedures to ensure the safety of the juveniles. Detention facilities should not be located in areas where there are known health or other hazards or risks.

33. Sleeping accommodation should normally consist of small group dormitories or individual bedrooms, while bearing in mind local standards. During sleeping hours there should be regular, unobtrusive supervision of all sleeping areas, including individual rooms and group dormitories, in order to ensure the protection of each juvenile. Every juvenile should, in accordance with local or national standards, be provided with separate and sufficient bedding, which should be clean when issued, kept in good order and changed often enough to ensure cleanliness.

34. Sanitary installations should be so located and of a sufficient standard to enable every juvenile to comply, as required, with their physical needs in privacy and in a clean and decent manner.

35. The possession of personal effects is a basic element of the right to privacy and essential to the psychological well-being of the juvenile. The right of every juvenile to possess personal effects and to have adequate storage facilities for them should be fully recognized and respected. Personal effects that the juvenile does not choose to retain or that are confiscated should be placed in safe custody. An inventory thereof should be signed by the juvenile. Steps should be taken to keep them in good condition. All such articles and money should be returned to the juvenile on release, except in so far as he or she has been authorized to spend money or send such property out of the facility. If a juvenile receives or is found in possession of any medicine, the medical officer should decide what use should be made of it.

36. To the extent possible juveniles should have the right to use their own clothing. Detention facilities should ensure that each juvenile has personal clothing suitable for the climate and adequate to ensure good health, and which should in no manner be degrading or humiliating. Juveniles removed from or leaving a facility for any purpose should be allowed to wear their own clothing.

37. Every detention facility shall ensure that every juvenile receives food that is suitably prepared and presented at normal meal times and of a quality and quantity to satisfy the standards of dietetics, hygiene and health and, as far as possible, religious and cultural requirements. Clean drinking water should be available to every juvenile at any time.

E. Education, vocational training and work

38. Every juvenile of compulsory school age has the right to education suited to his or her needs and abilities and designed to prepare him or her for return to society. Such education should be provided outside the detention facility in community schools wherever possible and, in any case, by qualified teachers through programmes integrated with the education system of the country so that, after release, juveniles may continue their education without difficulty. Special attention should be given by the administration of the detention facilities to the education of juveniles of foreign origin or with particular cultural or ethnic needs. Juveniles who are illiterate or have cognitive or learning difficulties should have the right to special education.

39. Juveniles above compulsory school age who wish to continue their education should be permitted and encouraged to do so, and every effort should be made to provide them with access to appropriate educational programmes.

40. Diplomas or educational certificates awarded to juveniles while in detention should not indicate in any way that the juvenile has been institutionalized.

41. Every detention facility should provide access to a library that is adequately stocked with both instructional and recreational books and periodicals suitable for the juveniles, who should be encouraged and enabled to make full use of it.
42. Every juvenile should have the right to receive vocational training in occupations likely to prepare him or her for future employment.
43. With due regard to proper vocational selection and to the requirements of institutional administration, juveniles should be able to choose the type of work they wish to perform.
44. All protective national and international standards applicable to child labor and young workers should apply to juveniles deprived of their liberty.
45. Wherever possible, juveniles should be provided with the opportunity to perform remunerated labor, if possible within the local community, as a complement to the vocational training provided in order to enhance the possibility of finding suitable employment when they return to their communities. The type of work should be such as to provide appropriate training that will be of benefit to the juveniles following release. The organization and methods of work offered in detention facilities should resemble as closely as possible those of similar work in the community, so as to prepare juveniles for the conditions of normal occupational life.
46. Every juvenile who performs work should have the right to an equitable remuneration. The interests of the juveniles and of their vocational training should not be subordinated to the purpose of making a profit for the detention facility or a third party. Part of the earnings of a juvenile should normally be set aside to constitute a savings fund to be handed over to the juvenile on release. The juvenile should have the right to use the remainder of those earnings to purchase articles for his or her own use or to indemnify the victim injured by his or her offense or to send it to his or her family or other persons outside the detention facility.

F. Recreation

47. Every juvenile should have the right to a suitable amount of time for daily free exercise, in the open air whenever weather permits, during which time appropriate recreational and physical training should normally be provided. Adequate space, installations and equipment should be provided for these activities. Every juvenile should have additional time for daily leisure activities, part of which should be devoted, if the juvenile so wishes, to arts and crafts skill development. The detention facility should ensure that each juvenile is physically able to participate in the available programmes of physical education. Remedial physical education and therapy should be offered, under medical supervision, to juveniles needing it.

G. Religion

48. Every juvenile should be allowed to satisfy the needs of his or her religious and spiritual life, in particular by attending the services or meetings provided in the detention facility or by conducting his or her own services and having possession of the necessary books or items of religious observance and instruction of his or her denomination. If a detention facility contains a sufficient number of juveniles of a given religion, one or more qualified representatives of that religion should be appointed or approved and allowed to hold regular services and to pay pastoral visits in private to juveniles at their request. Every juvenile should have the right to receive visits from a qualified representative of any religion of his or her choice, as well as the right not to participate in religious services and freely to decline religious education, counseling or indoctrination.

H. Medical care

49. Every juvenile shall receive adequate medical care, both preventive and remedial, including dental, ophthalmological and mental health care, as well as pharmaceutical products and special diets as medically indicated. All such medical care should, where possible, be provided to detained juveniles through the appropriate health facilities and services of the community in which the detention facility is located, in order to prevent stigmatization of the juvenile and promote self-respect and integration into the community.

50. Every juvenile has a right to be examined by a physician immediately upon admission to a detention facility, for the purpose of recording any evidence of prior ill-treatment and identifying any physical or mental condition requiring medical attention.

51. The medical services provided to juveniles should seek to detect and should treat any physical or mental illness, substance abuse or other condition that may hinder the integration of the juvenile into society. Every detention facility for juveniles should have immediate access to adequate medical facilities and equipment appropriate to the number and requirements of its residents and staff trained in preventive health care and the handling of medical emergencies. Every juvenile who is ill, who complains of illness or who demonstrates symptoms of physical or mental difficulties, should be examined promptly by a medical officer.

52. Any medical officer who has reason to believe that the physical or mental health of a juvenile has been or will be injuriously affected by continued detention, a hunger strike or any condition of detention should report this fact immediately to the director of the detention facility in question and to the independent authority responsible for safeguarding the well-being of the juvenile.

53. A juvenile who is suffering from mental illness should be treated in a specialized institution under independent medical management. Steps should be taken, by arrangement with appropriate agencies, to ensure any necessary continuation of mental health care after release.

54. Juvenile detention facilities should adopt specialized drug abuse prevention and rehabilitation programmes administered by qualified personnel. These programmes should be adapted to the age, sex and other requirements of the juveniles concerned, and detoxification facilities and services staffed by trained personnel should be available to drug- or alcohol-dependent juveniles.

55. Medicines should be administered only for necessary treatment on medical grounds and, when possible, after having obtained the informed consent of the juvenile concerned. In particular, they must not be administered with a view to eliciting information or a confession, as a punishment or as a means of restraint. Juveniles shall never be testers in the experimental use of drugs and treatment. The administration of any drug should always be authorized and carried out by qualified medical personnel.

I. Notification of illness, injury and death

56. The family or guardian of a juvenile and any other person designated by the juvenile have the right to be informed of the state of health of the juvenile on request and in the event of any important changes in the health of the juvenile. The director of the detention facility should notify immediately the family or guardian of the juvenile concerned, or other designated person, in case of death, illness requiring transfer of the juvenile to an outside medical facility, or a condition requiring clinical care within the detention facility for more than 48 hours. Notification should also be given to the consular authorities of the State of which a foreign juvenile is a citizen.

57. Upon the death of a juvenile during the period of deprivation of liberty, the nearest relative should have the right to inspect the death certificate, see the body and determine the method of disposal of the body. Upon the death of a juvenile in detention, there should be an independent inquiry into the causes of death, the report of which should be made accessible to the nearest relative. This inquiry should also be made when the death of a juvenile occurs within six months from the date of his or her release from the detention facility and there is reason to believe that the death is related to the period of detention.

58. A juvenile should be informed at the earliest possible time of the death, serious illness or injury of any immediate family member and should be provided with the opportunity to attend the funeral of the deceased or go to the bedside of a critically ill relative.

J. Contacts with the wider community

59. Every means should be provided to ensure that juveniles have adequate communication with the outside world, which is an integral part of the right to fair and humane treatment and is essential to the preparation of juveniles for their return to society. Juveniles should be allowed to communicate with their families, friends and other persons or representatives of reputable outside organizations, to leave detention facilities for a visit to their home and family and to receive special permission to leave the detention facility for educational, vocational or other important reasons. Should the juvenile be serving a sentence, the time spent outside a detention facility should be counted as part of the period of sentence.

60. Every juvenile should have the right to receive regular and frequent visits, in principle once a week and not less than once a month, in circumstances that respect the need of the juvenile for privacy, contact and unrestricted communication with the family and the defense counsel.

61. Every juvenile should have the right to communicate in writing or by telephone at least twice a week with the person of his or her choice, unless legally restricted, and should be assisted as necessary in order effectively to enjoy this right. Every juvenile should have the right to receive correspondence.

62. Juveniles should have the opportunity to keep themselves informed regularly of the news by reading newspapers, periodicals and other publications, through access to radio and television programmes and motion pictures, and through the visits of the representatives of any lawful club or organization in which the juvenile is interested.

K. Limitations of physical restraint and the use of force

63. Recourse to instruments of restraint and to force for any purpose should be prohibited, except as set forth in rule 64 below.

64. Instruments of restraint and force can only be used in exceptional cases, where all other control methods have been exhausted and failed, and only as explicitly authorized and specified by law and regulation. They should not cause humiliation or degradation, and should be used restrictively and only for the shortest possible period of time. By order of the director of the administration, such instruments might be resorted to in order to prevent the juvenile from inflicting self-injury, injuries to others or serious destruction of property. In such instances, the director should at once consult medical and other relevant personnel and report to the higher administrative authority.

65. The carrying and use of weapons by personnel should be prohibited in any facility where juveniles are detained.

L. Disciplinary procedures

66. Any disciplinary measures and procedures should maintain the interest of safety and an ordered community life and should be consistent with the upholding of the inherent dignity of the juvenile and the fundamental objective of institutional care, namely, instilling a sense of justice, self-respect and respect for the basic rights of every person.

67. All disciplinary measures constituting cruel, inhuman or degrading treatment shall be strictly prohibited, including corporal punishment, placement in a dark cell, closed or solitary confinement or any other punishment that may compromise the physical or mental health of the juvenile concerned. The reduction of diet and the restriction or denial of contact with family members should be prohibited for any purpose. Labor should always be viewed as an educational tool and a means of promoting the self-respect of the juvenile in preparing him or her for return to the community and should not be imposed as a disciplinary sanction. No juvenile should be sanctioned more than once for the same disciplinary infraction. Collective sanctions should be prohibited.

68. Legislation or regulations adopted by the competent administrative authority should establish norms concerning the following, taking full account of the fundamental characteristics, needs and rights of juveniles:

　(a) Conduct constituting a disciplinary offense;
　(b) Type and duration of disciplinary sanctions that may be inflicted;
　(c) The authority competent to impose such sanctions;
　(d) The authority competent to consider appeals.

69. A report of misconduct should be presented promptly to the competent authority, which should decide on it without undue delay. The competent authority should conduct a thorough examination of the case.

70. No juvenile should be disciplinarily sanctioned except in strict accordance with the terms of the law and regulations in force. No juvenile should be sanctioned unless he or she has been informed of the alleged infraction in a manner appropriate to the full understanding of the juvenile, and given a proper opportunity of presenting his or her defense, including the right of appeal to a competent impartial authority. Complete records should be kept of all disciplinary proceedings.

71. No juveniles should be responsible for disciplinary functions except in the supervision of specified social, educational or sports activities or in self-government programmes.

M. Inspection and complaints

72. Qualified inspectors or an equivalent duly constituted authority not belonging to the administration of the facility should be empowered to conduct inspections on a regular basis and to undertake unannounced inspections on their own initiative, and should enjoy full guarantees of independence in the exercise of this function. Inspectors should have unrestricted access to all persons employed by or working in any facility where juveniles are or may be deprived of their liberty, to all juveniles and to all records of such facilities.

73. Qualified medical officers attached to the inspecting authority or the public health service should participate in the inspections, evaluating compliance with the rules concerning the physical environment, hygiene, accommodation, food, exercise and medical services, as well as any other aspect or conditions of institutional life that affect the physical and mental health of juveniles. Every juvenile should have the right to talk in confidence to any inspecting officer.

74. After completing the inspection, the inspector should be required to submit a report on the findings. The report should include an evaluation of the compliance of the detention facilities with the present rules and relevant provisions of national law, and recommendations regarding any steps considered necessary to ensure compliance with them. Any facts discovered by an inspector that appear to indicate that a violation of legal provisions concerning the rights of juveniles or the operation of a juvenile detention facility has occurred should be communicated to the competent authorities for investigation and prosecution.

75. Every juvenile should have the opportunity of making requests or complaints to the director of the detention facility and to his or her authorized representative.

76. Every juvenile should have the right to make a request or complaint, without censorship as to substance, to the central administration, the judicial authority or other proper authorities through approved channels, and to be informed of the response without delay.

77. Efforts should be made to establish an independent office (ombudsman) to receive and investigate complaints made by juveniles deprived of their liberty and to assist in the achievement of equitable settlements.

78. Every juvenile should have the right to request assistance from family members, legal counselors, humanitarian groups or others where possible, in order to make a complaint. Illiterate juveniles should be provided with assistance should they need to use the services of public or private agencies and organizations which provide legal counsel or which are competent to receive complaints.

N. *Return to the community*

79. All juveniles should benefit from arrangements designed to assist them in returning to society, family life, education or employment after release. Procedures, including early release, and special courses should be devised to this end.

80. Competent authorities should provide or ensure services to assist juveniles in re-establishing themselves in society and to lessen prejudice against such juveniles. These services should ensure', to the extent possible, that the juvenile is provided with suitable residence, employment, clothing, and sufficient means to maintain himself or herself upon release in order to facilitate successful reintegration. The representatives of agencies providing such services should be consulted and should have access to juveniles while detained, with a view to assisting them in their return to the community.

V. Personnel

81. Personnel should be qualified and include a sufficient number of specialists such as educators, vocational instructors, counselors, social workers, psychiatrists and psychologists. These and other specialist staff should normally be employed on a permanent basis. This should not preclude part-time or volunteer workers when the level of support and training they can provide is appropriate and beneficial. Detention facilities should make use of all remedial, educational, moral, spiritual, and other resources and forms of assistance that are appropriate and available in the community, according to the individual needs and problems of detained juveniles.

82. The administration should provide for the careful selection and recruitment of every grade and type of personnel, since the proper management of detention facilities depends on their integrity, humanity, ability and professional capacity to deal with juveniles, as well as personal suitability for the work.

83. To secure the foregoing ends, personnel should be appointed as professional officers with adequate remuneration to attract and retain suitable women and men. The personnel of juvenile detention facilities should be continually encouraged to fulfil their duties and obligations in a humane, committed, professional, fair and efficient manner, to conduct themselves at all times in such a way as to deserve and gain the respect of the juveniles, and to provide juveniles with a positive role model and perspective.

84. The administration should introduce forms of organization and management that facilitate communications between different categories of staff in each detention facility so as to enhance cooperation between the various services engaged in the care of juveniles, as well as between staff and the administration,

with a view to ensuring that staff directly in contact with juveniles are able to function in conditions favorable to the efficient fulfilment of their duties.

85. The personnel should receive such training as will enable them to carry out their responsibilities effectively, in particular training in child psychology, child welfare and international standards and norms of human rights and the rights of the child, including the present Rules. The personnel should maintain and improve their knowledge and professional capacity by attending courses of in-service training, to be organized at suitable intervals throughout their career.

86. The director of a facility should be adequately qualified for his or her task, with administrative ability and suitable training and experience, and should carry out his or her duties on a full-time basis.

87. In the performance of their duties, personnel of detention facilities should respect and protect the human dignity and fundamental human rights of all juveniles, in particular, as follows:

(a) No member of the detention facility or institutional personnel may inflict, instigate or tolerate any act of torture or any form of harsh, cruel, inhuman or degrading treatment, punishment, correction or discipline under any pretext or circumstance whatsoever;

(b) All personnel should rigorously oppose and combat any act of corruption, reporting it without delay to the competent authorities;

(c) All personnel should respect the present Rules. Personnel who have reason to believe that a serious violation of the present Rules has occurred or is about to occur should report the matter to their superior authorities or organs vested with reviewing or remedial power;

(d) All personnel should ensure the full protection of the physical and mental health of juveniles, including protection from physical, sexual and emotional abuse and exploitation, and should take immediate action to secure medical attention whenever required;

(e) All personnel should respect the right of the juvenile to privacy, and, in particular, should safeguard all confidential matters concerning juveniles or their families learned as a result of their professional capacity;

(f) All personnel should seek to minimize any differences between life inside and outside the detention facility which tend to lessen due respect for the dignity of juveniles as human beings.

APPENDIX D:

U.N. Code of Conduct For Law Enforcement Officials

U.N. Code of Conduct for Law Enforcement Officials, G.A. res. 34/169, annex, 34 U.N. GAOR Supp. (No. 46) at 186, U.N. Doc. A/34/46 (1979).

Article 1

Law enforcement officials shall at all times fulfil the duty imposed upon them by law, by serving the community and by protecting all persons against illegal acts, consistent with the high degree of responsibility required by their profession.

Commentary:
(a) The term "law enforcement officials', includes all officers of the law, whether appointed or elected, who exercise police powers, especially the powers of arrest or detention.

(b) In countries where police powers are exercised by military authorities, whether uniformed or not, or by State security forces, the definition of law enforcement officials shall be regarded as including officers of such services.

(c) Service to the community is intended to include particularly the rendition of services of assistance to those members of the community who by reason of personal, economic, social or other emergencies are in need of immediate aid.

(d) This provision is intended to cover not only all violent, predatory and harmful acts, but extends to the full range of prohibitions under penal statutes. It extends to conduct by persons not capable of incurring criminal liability.

Article 2

In the performance of their duty, law enforcement officials shall respect and protect human dignity and maintain and uphold the human rights of all persons.

Commentary:
(a) The human rights in question are identified and protected by national and international law. Among the relevant international instruments are the Universal Declaration of Human Rights, the International Covenant on Civil and Political Rights, the Declaration on the Protection of All Persons from Being Subjected to

Torture and Other Cruel, Inhuman or Degrading Treatment or Punishment, the United Nations Declaration on the Elimination of All Forms of Racial Discrimination, the International Convention on the Elimination of All Forms of Racial Discrimination, the International Convention on the Suppression and Punishment of the Crime of Apartheid, the Convention on the Prevention and Punishment of the Crime of Genocide, the Standard Minimum Rules for the Treatment of Prisoners and the Vienna Convention on Consular Relations.

(b) National commentaries to this provision should indicate regional or national provisions identifying and protecting these rights.

Article 3

Law enforcement officials may use force only when strictly necessary and to the extent required for the performance of their duty.

Commentary:

(a) This provision emphasizes that the use of force by law enforcement officials should be exceptional; while it implies that law enforcement officials may be authorized to use force as is reasonably necessary under the circumstances for theprevention of crime or in effecting or assisting in the lawful arrest of offenders or suspected offenders, no force going beyond that may be used.

(b) National law ordinarily restricts the use of force by law enforcement officials in accordance with a principle of proportionality. It is to be understood that such national principles of proportionality are to be respected in the interpretation of this provision. In no case should this
provision be interpreted to authorize the use of force which is disproportionate to the legitimate objective to be achieved.

(c) The use of firearms is considered an extreme measure. Every effort should be made to exclude the use of firearms, especially against children. In general, firearms should not be used except when a suspected offender offers armed resistance or otherwise jeopardizes the lives of others and less extreme measures are not sufficient to restrain or apprehend the suspected offender. In every instance in which a firearm is discharged, a report should be made promptly to the competent authorities.

rticle 4

Matters of a confidential nature in the possession of law enforcement officials shall be kept confidential, unless the performance of duty or the needs of justice strictly require otherwise.

Commentary:
By the nature of their duties, law enforcement officials obtain information which may relate to private lives or be potentially harmful to the interests, and especially the reputation, of others. Great care should be exercised in safeguarding and using such information, which should be disclosed only in the performance of duty or to serve the needs of justice. Any disclosure of such information for other purposes is wholly improper.

Article 5

No law enforcement official may inflict, instigate or tolerate any act of torture or other cruel, inhuman or degrading treatment or punishment, nor may any law enforcement official invoke superior orders or exceptional circumstances such as a state of war or a threat of war, a threat to national security, internal political instability or any other public emergency as a
justification of torture or other cruel, inhuman or degrading treatment or punishment.

Commentary:
(a) This prohibition derives from the Declaration on the Protection of All Persons from Being Subjected to Torture and Other Cruel, Inhuman or Degrading Treatment or Punishment, adopted by the General Assembly, according to which:

"[Such an act is] an offense to human dignity and shall be condemned as a denial of the purposes of the Charter of the United Nations and as a violation of the human rights and fundamental freedoms proclaimed in the Universal Declaration of Human Rights [and other international human rights instruments]."

(b) The Declaration defines torture as follows:

"... torture means any act by which severe pain or suffering, whether physical or mental, is intentionally inflicted by or at the instigation of a public official on a person for such purposes as obtaining from him or a third person information or confession, punishing him for an act he has committed or is suspected of having committed, or intimidating him or other persons. It does not include pain or suffering arising only from, inherent in or incidental to, lawful sanctions to the extent consistent with the Standard Minimum Rules for the Treatment of Prisoners."

(c) The term "cruel, inhuman or degrading treatment or punishment" has not been defined by the General Assembly but should be interpreted so as to extend the widest possible protection against abuses, whether physical or mental.

Article 6

Law enforcement officials shall ensure the full protection of the health of persons in their custody and, in particular, shall take immediate action to secure medical attention whenever required.

Commentary:
(a) "Medical attention", which refers to services rendered by any medical personnel, including certified medical practitioners and paramedics, shall be secured when needed or requested.

(b) While the medical personnel are likely to be attached to the law enforcement operation, law enforcement officials must take into account the judgement of such personnel when they recommend providing the person in custody with appropriate treatment through, or in consultation with, medical personnel from outside the law enforcement operation.

(c) It is understood that law enforcement officials shall also secure medical attention for victims of violations of law or of accidents occurring in the course of violations of law.

Article 7

Law enforcement officials shall not commit any act of corruption. They shall also rigorously oppose and combat all such acts.

Commentary:
(a) Any act of corruption, in the same way as any other abuse of authority, is incompatible with the profession of law enforcement officials. The law must be

enforced fully with respect to any law enforcement official who commits an act of corruption, as Governments cannot expect to enforce the law among their citizens if they cannot, or will not, enforce the law against their own agents and within their agencies.

(b) While the definition of corruption must be subject to national law, it should be understood to encompass the commission or omission of an act in the performance of or in connection with one's duties, in response to gifts, promises or incentives demanded or accepted, or the wrongful receipt of these once the act has been committed or omitted.

(c) The expression "act of corruption" referred to above should be understood to encompass attempted corruption.

Article 8

Law enforcement officials shall respect the law and the present Code. They shall also, to the best of their capability, prevent and rigorously oppose any violations of them.

Law enforcement officials who have reason to believe that a violation of the present Code has occurred or is about to occur shall report the matter to their superior authorities and, where necessary, to other appropriate authorities or organs vested with reviewing or remedial power.

Commentary:
(a) This Code shall be observed whenever it has been incorporated into national legislation or practice. If legislation or practice contains stricter provisions than those of the present Code, those stricter provisions shall be observed.

(b) The article seeks to preserve the balance between the need for internal discipline of the agency on which public safety is largely dependent, on the one hand, and the need for dealing with violations of basic human rights, on the other. Law enforcement officials shall report violations within the chain of command and take other lawful action outside the chain of command only when no other remedies are available or effective. It is understood that law enforcement officials shall not suffer administrative or other penalties because they have reported that a violation of this Code has occurred or is about to occur.

(c) The term "appropriate authorities or organs vested with reviewing or remedial power" refers to any authority or organ existing under national law, whether internal to the law enforcement agency or independent thereof, with statutory, customary or other power to review grievances and complaints arising out of violations within the purview of this Code.

(d) In some countries, the mass media may be regarded as performing complaint review functions similar to those described in subparagraph (c) above. Law enforcement officials may, therefore, be justified if, as a last resort and in accordance with the laws and customs of their own countries and with the provisions of article 4 of the present Code, they bring violations to the attention of public opinion through the mass media.

(e) Law enforcement officials who comply with the provisions of this Code deserve the respect, the full support and the co-operation of the community and of the law enforcement agency in which they serve, as well as the law enforcement profession.

APPENDIX E:

U.N. Basic Principles on The Use of Force And Firearms by Law Enforcement Officials

U.N. Basic Principles on the Use of Force and Firearms by Law Enforcement Officials, Eighth U.N. Congress on the Prevention of Crime and the Treatment of Offenders, Havana, 27 August to 7 September 1990, U.N. Doc. A/CONF.144/28/Rev.1 at 112 (1990).

Whereas the work of law enforcement officials* is a social service of great importance and there is, therefore, a need to maintain and, whenever necessary, to improve the working conditions and status of these officials,

Whereas a threat to the life and safety of law enforcement officials must be seen as a threat to the stability of society as a whole,

Whereas law enforcement officials have a vital role in the protection of the right to life, liberty and security of the person, as guaranteed in the Universal Declaration of Human Rights and reaffirmed in the International Covenant on Civil and Political Rights,

Whereas the Standard Minimum Rules for the Treatment of Prisoners provide for the circumstances in which prison officials may use force in the course of their duties,

Whereas article 3 of the Code of Conduct for Law Enforcement Officials provides that law enforcement officials may use force only when strictly necessary and to the extent required for the performance of their duty,

Whereas the preparatory meeting for the Seventh United Nations Congress on the Prevention of Crime and the Treatment of Offenders, held at Varenna, Italy, agreed on elements to be considered in the course of further work on restraints on the use of force and firearms by law enforcement officials,

Whereas the Seventh Congress, in its resolution 14, inter alia, emphasizes that the use of force and firearms by law enforcement officials should be commensurate with due respect for human rights,

Whereas the Economic and Social Council, in its resolution 1986/10, section IX, of 21 May 1986, invited Member States to pay particular attention in the implementation of the Code to the use of force and firearms by law enforcement officials, and the General Assembly, in its resolution 41/149 of 4 December 1986, inter alia, welcomed this recommendation made by the Council, Whereas it is appropriate that, with due regard to their personal safety, consideration be given to the role of law enforcement officials in relation to the administration of justice, to the protection of the right to life, liberty and security of the person, to their responsibility to maintain public safety and social peace and to the importance of their qualifications, training and conduct,

The basic principles set forth below, which have been formulated to assist Member States in their task of ensuring and promoting the proper role of law enforcement officials, should be taken into account and respected by Governments within the framework of their national legislation and practice, and be brought to the attention of law enforcement officials as well as other persons, such as judges, prosecutors, lawyers, members of the executive branch and the legislature, and the public.

General provisions

1. Governments and law enforcement agencies shall adopt and implement rules and regulations on the use of force and firearms against persons by law enforcement officials. In developing such rules and regulations, Governments and law enforcement agencies shall keep the ethical issues associated with the use of force and firearms constantly under review.

2. Governments and law enforcement agencies should develop a range of means as broad as possible and equip law enforcement officials with various types of weapons and ammunition that would allow for a differentiated use of force and firearms. These should include the development of non-lethal incapacitating weapons for use in appropriate situations, with a view to increasingly restraining the application of means capable of causing death or injury to persons. For the same purpose, it should also be possible for law enforcement officials to be equipped with self-defensive equipment such as shields, helmets, bullet-proof vests

and bullet-proof means of transportation, in order to decrease the need to use weapons of any kind.

3. The development and deployment of non-lethal incapacitating weapons should be carefully evaluated in order to minimize the risk of endangering uninvolved persons, and the use of such weapons should be carefully controlled.

4. Law enforcement officials, in carrying out their duty, shall, as far as possible, apply non-violent means before resorting to the use of force and firearms. They may use force and firearms only if other means remain ineffective or without any promise of achieving the intended result.

5. Whenever the lawful use of force and firearms is unavoidable, law enforcement officials shall:

(a) Exercise restraint in such use and act in proportion to the seriousness of the offense and the legitimate objective to be achieved;

(b) Minimize damage and injury, and respect and preserve human life;

(c) Ensure that assistance and medical aid are rendered to any injured or affected persons at the earliest possible moment;

(d) Ensure that relatives or close friends of the injured or affected person are notified at the earliest possible moment.

6. Where injury or death is caused by the use of force and firearms by law enforcement officials, they shall report the incident promptly to their superiors, in accordance with principle 22.

7. Governments shall ensure that arbitrary or abusive use of force and firearms by law enforcement officials is punished as a criminal offense under their law.

8. Exceptional circumstances such as internal political instability or any other public emergency may not be invoked to justify any departure from these basic principles.

Special provisions

9. Law enforcement officials shall not use firearms against persons except in self-defense or defense of others against the imminent threat of death or serious injury, to prevent the perpetration of a particularly serious crime involving grave threat to life, to arrest a person presenting such a danger and resisting their authority, or to prevent his or her escape, and only when less extreme means are insufficient to achieve these objectives. In any event, intentional lethal use of firearms may only be made when strictly unavoidable in order to protect life.

10. In the circumstances provided for under principle 9, law enforcement officials shall identify themselves as such and give a clear warning of their intent to use firearms, with sufficient time for the warning to be observed, unless to do so would unduly place the law enforcement officials at risk or would create a risk of death or serious harm to other persons, or would be clearly inappropriate or pointless in the circumstances of the incident.

11. Rules and regulations on the use of firearms by law enforcement officials should include guidelines that:

(a) Specify the circumstances under which law enforcement officials are authorized to carry firearms and prescribe the types of firearms and ammunition permitted;

(b) Ensure that firearms are used only in appropriate circumstances and in a manner likely to decrease the risk of unnecessary harm;

(c) Prohibit the use of those firearms and ammunition that cause unwarranted injury or present an unwarranted risk;

(d) Regulate the control, storage and issuing of firearms, including procedures for ensuring that law enforcement officials are accountable for the firearms and ammunition issued to them;

(e) Provide for warnings to be given, if appropriate, when firearms are to be discharged;

(f) Provide for a system of reporting whenever law enforcement officials use firearms in the performance of their duty.

Policing unlawful assemblies

12. As everyone is allowed to participate in lawful and peaceful assemblies, in accordance with the principles embodied in the Universal Declaration of Human Rights and the International Covenant on Civil and Political Rights, Governments and law enforcement agencies and officials shall recognize that force and firearms may be used only in accordance with principles 13 and 14.

13. In the dispersal of assemblies that are unlawful but non-violent, law enforcement officials shall avoid the use of force or, where that is not practicable, shall restrict such force to the minimum extent necessary.

14. In the dispersal of violent assemblies, law enforcement officials may use firearms only when less dangerous means are not practicable and only to the minimum extent necessary. Law enforcement officials shall not use firearms in such cases, except under the conditions stipulated in principle 9.

Policing persons in custody or detention

15. Law enforcement officials, in their relations with persons in custody or detention, shall not use force, except when strictly necessary for the maintenance of security and order within the institution, or when personal safety is threatened.

16. Law enforcement officials, in their relations with persons in custody or detention, shall not use firearms, except in self-defense or in the defense of others against the immediate threat of death or serious injury, or when strictly necessary to prevent the escape of a person in custody or detention presenting the danger referred to in principle 9.

17. The preceding principles are without prejudice to the rights, duties and responsibilities of prison officials, as set out in the Standard Minimum Rules for the Treatment of Prisoners, particularly rules 33, 34 and 54.

Qualifications, training and counseling

18. Governments and law enforcement agencies shall ensure that all law enforcement officials are selected by proper screening procedures, have appropriate moral, psychological and physical qualities for the effective exercise of their

functions and receive continuous and thorough professional training. Their continued fitness to perform these functions should be subject to periodic review.

19. Governments and law enforcement agencies shall ensure that all law enforcement officials are provided with training and are tested in accordance with appropriate proficiency standards in the use of force. Those law enforcement officials who are required to carry firearms should be authorized to do so only upon completion of special training in their use.

20. In the training of law enforcement officials, Governments and law enforcement agencies shall give special attention to issues of police ethics and human rights, especially in the investigative process, to alternatives to the use of force and firearms, including the peaceful settlement of conflicts, the understanding of crowd behavior, and the methods of persuasion, negotiation and mediation, as well as to technical means, with a view to limiting the use of force and firearms. Law enforcement agencies should review their training programmes and operational procedures in the light of particular incidents.

21. Governments and law enforcement agencies shall make stress counseling available to law enforcement officials who are involved in situations where force and firearms are used.

Reporting and review procedures

22. Governments and law enforcement agencies shall establish effective reporting and review procedures for all incidents referred to in principles 6 and 11 (f). For incidents reported pursuant to these principles, Governments and law enforcement agencies shall ensure that an effective review process is available and that independent administrative or prosecutorial authorities are in a position to exercise jurisdiction in appropriate circumstances. In cases of death and serious injury or other grave consequences, a detailed report shall be sent promptly to the competent authorities responsible for administrative review and judicial control.

23. Persons affected by the use of force and firearms or their legal representatives shall have access to an independent process, including a judicial process. In the event of the death of such persons, this provision shall apply to their dependants accordingly.

24. Governments and law enforcement agencies shall ensure that superior officers are held responsible if they know, or should have known, that law enforcement officials under their command are resorting, or have resorted, to the unlawful use of force and firearms, and they did not take all measures in their power to prevent, suppress or report such use.

25. Governments and law enforcement agencies shall ensure that no criminal or disciplinary sanction is imposed on law enforcement officials who, in compliance with the Code of Conduct for Law Enforcement Officials and these basic principles, refuse to carry out an order to use force and firearms, or who report such use by other officials.

26. Obedience to superior orders shall be no defense if law enforcement officials knew that an order to use force and firearms resulting in the death or serious injury of a person was manifestly unlawful and had a reasonable opportunity to refuse to follow it. In any case, responsibility also rests on the superiors who gave the unlawful orders.

---

* In accordance with the commentary to article 1 of the Code of Conduct for Law Enforcement Officials, the term "law enforcement officials" includes all officers of the law, whether appointed or elected, who exercise police powers, especially the powers of arrest or detention. In countries where police powers are exercised by military authorities. whether uniformed or not, or by State security forces, the definition of law enforcement officials shall be regarded as including officers of such services.